NOTICE

STOP

Help Save The Youth of America
DON'T BUY NEGRO RECORDS

(If you don't want to serve negroes in your place of business, then do not have negro records on your juke box or listen to negro records on the radio.)

The screaming, idiotic words, and savage music of these records are undermining the morals of our white youth in America.

Call the advertisers of the radio stations that play this type of music and complain to them!

Don't Let Your Children Buy, or Listen
To These Negro Records

For additional copies of this circular, write
CITIZENS' COUNCIL OF GREATER NEW ORLEANS, INC.
509 Delta Building   New Orleans Louisiana 70112

Permission is granted to re-print this circular

Concept by Harmony Holiday
Design and layout by Harmony Holiday and Rebecca Wolff

Published in the United States by Fence Books
Science Library, 320
University at Albany
1400 Washington Avenue, Albany, NY 12222

www.fenceportal.org

This book was printed by Versa Press
and distributed by Small Press Distribution
and Consortium Book Sales and Distribution.

Library of Congress Cataloguing in Publication Data
Holiday, Harmony [1982–]
Hollywood Forever/Harmony Holiday

Library of Congress Control Number: 2017930668

ISBN 13: 978-0-9864373-0-4

First Edition

10 9 8 7 6 5 4 3 2

Harmony Holiday

THE GUARDIAN

Manchester   Monday July 1 1968

Martin Luther King's mother slain in church

From HENRY WINCHESTER, Washington, June 30

A Space warning from Sun Ra to the Planet Earth

The redeemer said she was covered
with the blood of wolves   who had tried
to consume the lamb.

There is a beauty aloof from struggle but there's also this need in
me to call out on radios and video tape   what's your slave name,
what's your slave name 'til both sides buckle and fold from their
knees sobbing and wailing and then the sound dims just enough to
make everyone look like a ghetto mystic tumbling across his own
shadow into this fix of vogue

There is a house in new orleans
They call it   the rising sun

Early in the freedom I found my crow, my crown, my why come.

People who are moving ard will have to get together nove forward rs. Everybody who is of good ind constructive....got to pull nd unify and *build!*....accord- what they nee ow they need help on this t, because of the fact that ior forces have turned the tions around on that set in a direction for them. Every man ought to telligent enough bad things that are happening manity are not are designed and planned and, rinted. Now all e that keep on warning man.... re going to tell me that he's to sleep thru all that. What I people do if an army of bees ced them intelligently and tly? If they keep on being out der with Nature, and r insects and birds will get out der too. Something n from the skies and kill every- on this planet, and there won't othing they can do about it. ning whatsoever. If fire rained n from Heaven, there won't be kind of defense. If the water up on th , there won't nse whatsoever. Every now and Nature throws out these warn-

ings. Like the birds who flew into one of the tallest buildings in New into that building and fell down to the ground. Now you know that birds are not supposed to do that. They lot of places, bees are biting folks. bees have crawled up men's pants supposed to do nothing like that. Seas got hounds and rivers got the same man. He is not supposed to be rising does, the other forces will do the When I read the History of human beings I don't see no progress. Every thing is standing still....like humanity is on a treadmill, just walking and walking and walking, and the faster they walk the tireder they get, and getting anywhere. They should see the scenery changes, but it's still the same old dull scenery....and nothing changes. They say History repeats itself. If it repeats itself then nobody is getting anywhere if the History itself is no good. It's tory is bad....and it's bad all right. It's worse than anything any

writer could write about. Of all the schools they got and all the philosophies sent to them. It's not supposed to be like that on this planet....but you see, it is. So they can't blame the men who gave up their time to Science and offerings for Humanity and all the les they made....sacrificing all their pleasures, doing without Sake of people. All that time those the men who went to war, who died for a better World....died in vain. Now the Creator of the Universe doesn't like anything like that, and this planet will be penalised far beyond its endurance if it is not careful. Not only will it be penalised, it will be eliminated out of the Solar System, because it is not serving any useful purpose. If a planet gets so that it's no use to its own self....it can't be any use to the Creator of the Universe. If people get so that they are no use to their own selves, then how can they be of any use to the Creator....or to anything. Yet it has reached that point and it is a very of lives are at stake at this point in a way which has never been like this before, because this is another Age

that people are living in, and Codes are different than in t that has just gone by. But yo they are still over there in th thinking that they can achie thing with the same rules the don't expect folks ne in to Greater Natu not talking about Nature on Greater Nature of the Univer always in tune. Nature is like This planet is lik instrument. Instruments get d when they do the person to tune it is really a M musician. He's got the natur and knows how it is suppose sound. It's just like on a pia you've got all the G's out of you can arrange the scaling a nobody is going to miss that you took out. You can add f notes or you can do some mo to five notes. You can chang and so can the Creator. He is musician too you know. He planet keeps on being out of can kick it right out of the o You have heard about the m the spheres; that's what it m Every planet is a sphere and . This o on the note of G right now. it's not supposed to be G, b named itself G. via Pat Griffi

WHO ARE THE REAL BLACK SUPERSTARS?

I want a land where the sun kills questions

You've got a White chauffeur, a yacht, and the key to the executive washroom! You've got it made. Right? Wrong! —A NEW LOOK AT BLACKS AT THE TOP

Get it how you live, son   Jezebel Said

It's common to feel illumination from within, as if thousands of little lights were burning inside your body. Flat fiction of a race trapped in the stupor of transcendence

Here's this unidentified, but identifiable for some, black man, walking out of a dingy, ominously lenient jail cell, his suit covered in blood, head bandaged, eyes downcast in arrogance before shame or arrogant shame, and he has his impeccably clad high yellow woman in his arms, and she's gripping his bloodied coat in a gesture of infinite nearness and we can't tell whether she's sobbing or grinning.

Rejoice. We have lost track of the difference. Between voyeurism and the clan (see The Mirror's Guide to the Cults). Does it matter that the man is Miles Davis, the woman his exquisite first wife, Frances Taylor, a principal dancer for Alvin Ailey. Does it matter that earlier this same night Miles had a gig at the Village Vanguard, and stepped out between sets for a cigarette. Is style a killer. Does it matter that while he was smoking a cop walked up to him and called him a nigger, said he couldn't stand in front of this white-man's establishment and flaunt his beauty and what was he thinking, sincerely, the NYPD.

This cop was not aware that Miles was headlining the night's show so Miles let him know, pointed to the marquee, calm, not moving from his position in front of the Vanguard. This angered the officer, slurred his envy, and the exchange escalated until he took a sudden billy club to the trumpeter's head, knocked him ready.

This is an autopsy of that event, across eras and causes. This image/ document is our refrain and our excess, embattled, reconciling one another, bloody and wiser, the tonic that occupies our hearts whenever we dance in the risk of showmanship with private intentions.. And all innocence is wilderness. And the man leaving the jail cell has a fresh cigarette between his lips, crackling and burning. And on the edge of the scene there's this semi-limp white hand coiled around our dreams.

This was yesterday. This is tomorrow. Clichés so patient they become subtle, surreal, and sublime, make the unsung elegance of tabloids. Of everything we wanted to know that wasn't our business but could save our lives. We call on Hollywood as a vector toward the resensualizing of the imaginary. As a space of both victory and sorrow for the lost black hero who is villain who is star, whose archives are lost or unlisted. He is lost, she is lost, with them.

I've come here to lash out
I've come here to reclaim my tenderness
Which is not linear and I'm trying to remember
the white mink coat I wore on the plantation, but it all fades to war paint and we wake up
in Los Angeles

His isn't a vacant smile but it leaks rage and lazy insight
Mine isn't a shattered praise but it returns   aloof from the dream reciprocal and we
still wake up
in Los Angeles

We hit the pitched Iowa road like convicts in his landless motor   saw a white god in
Texas and black one in shackles   and we still woke up in Los Angeles   the choked
up mecca of our carbon black masks   this fame   that ass   etcetera

Put the good brand on television   with   a live studio audience   watching him repeat
the same rehearsed affection   to sell   beer and candy   And right in the middle of
my laugh I felt this crazy   urge to cry

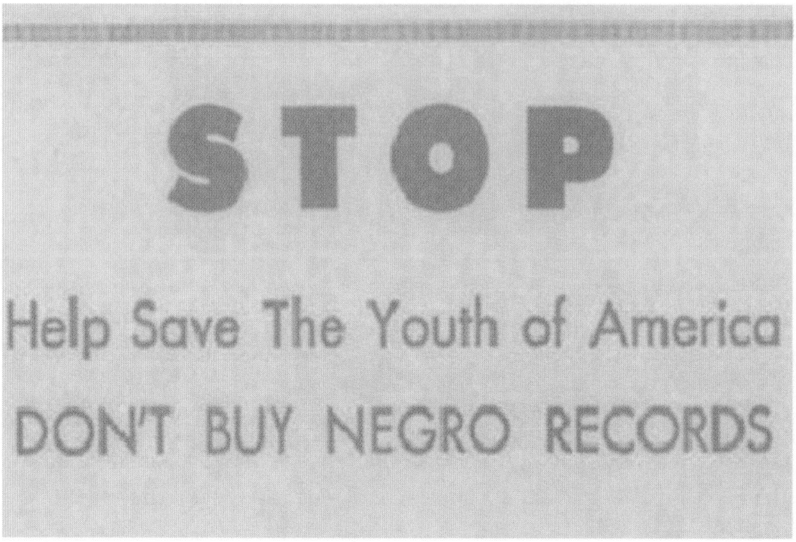
STOP
Help Save The Youth of America
DON'T BUY NEGRO RECORDS

Adultery

Dr. Martin Luther King Jr.

FUNERAL SERVICES

Ebenezer Baptist Church, April 9, 1968

The adventure that you're ready for is the one that you get. What's sad
about that. Let's!   Make it great.

Even MLK. He stepped out onto the balcony for a private cigarette after
sex with a woman who wasn't his wife (so what) (does that make him)
when they shot him

PLUS

in the heart Great Speeches
right /then?

I'VE BEEN TO THE

The sex and the death are unrelated   except   both MOUNTAIN TOP
relieve the pressure of his quiet wish   to be

I HAVE A DREAM
saved
HISTORIC ADDRESS
MADE AT
THE MARCH ON
WASHINGTON, D. C.
AUG. 28, 1963

Is our savior vulgar
The wish for rescue, is it vulgar
Is grace itself, too, vulgar?

Do you want your oppressor to save you, too / Who else
could do it? So beautifully his blue duty be

Men are never   white blackbirds™

MARTIN LUTHER KING....AT
COMMUNIST TRAINING SCHOOL

Is this tomorrow?

And the new mythology begins to love me

With an immediacy that seems at once artless and profoundly sophisticated.
You mean one sweet sin could bring freedom everlasting, for our king.
That's our King! Those sirens his baffled cheering, all vague and precise like
an unmarked gravesite that might be his own, but he had another name for
his disappearance   he   called it   f a i t h   one shade past   fate   eventfully
shattered with a grasp of it. A savior's safety. And then he got his wish.
And then we / at last   listened.   I heard black people don't get depressed,
besides as performance. And the Bible says. What's popular now is the way
the miracle of pure style cures or is it curses—cross our hearts with jive
nerve and hopes to hide of what it don't get   while new brand

angels sing hexes into bottles of northern comfort. Uproar. Jesus! Already
these myths are obsolete too and fresh the cold details he was bleeding his
twisted love into.

He was bleeding his twisted love. He was bleeding his twisted love. He was
bleeding his twisted love. He is bleeding his   twisted   love

The above picture was made by an employee of the State of Georgia at the Highlander
Folk School in Monteagle, Tennessee during the Labor Day week-end of 1957. A photo-
grapher was sent to the Highlander Folk School by the Georgia Commission on Education.
The Highlander Folk School was abolished by an act of the Legislature of the State of Ten-
nessee at a later date because it was charged with being a subversive organization.

Those attending were:

1. Martin Luther King, Jr., of the Montgomery, Alabama, and Albany, Georgia riots. Karl
Prussion, a counterspy for the FBI for twenty-two years, charges that Martin Luther King
belongs to sixty Communist-front organizations — more than any Communist in the
United States. He is promoted and encouraged by the Kennedys.

2. Abner W. Berry of the Central Committee of the Communist Party.

3. Aubrey Williams, President of the Southern Conference Education Fund, Inc., The Trans-
mission Belt in the South for the Communist Party.

4. Myles Horton, Director of Highlander Folk School for Communist Training, Monteagle,
Tennessee.

These "Four Horsemen" of racial agitation have brought tension, disturbance, strife
and violence in their advancement of the Communist doctrine of "racial nationalism."

JOIN THE AUGUSTA COURIER IN THE FIGHT FOR FREEDOM

You don't know

And that's how slaughter become a thought away

from the warmest shame in all our hearts

what love is

NEGROES

BEWARE

That's Entertainment:

DO NOT ATTEND

A crisis of rumors resolved by what they cover for. You know when you're watching a
favorite movie and keep rewinding to the part before your hero is killed. That's Black
American immortality. MLK is dangling his American Spirit in one hand. Some Memphis
fancy canopy gesture with the other, about hunger, his human hunger. His mistress is
downstairs fixing her hair for dinner, buzzing with the spirals he's just carved into her.
Jesse Jackson and them are in the courtyard just beneath Martin's motel room balcony,
allowing him to falcon for them, dressed like dandies and value systems, the black
middle class minority, huddled around duskdreams of spirituals and pigs' feet as all
the doves break free. Why are there guns in these pianos. Bystanders gasping off-key.
As the shot strokes his soul   he begs Byard to sing   him Stevie Wonder   from the
future sequence is over   please tell your story/ faster   if you don't it will come to
pass— sure, we used to be naïve and think we could live without killing, but lately,

               In his breast pocket a note about ritual   sacrifice, bloodied,
  · his witch doctor's advice / phone number   Heaven's only for the sinners

COMMUNIST
MEETINGS

Paid organizers for the communists are
only trying to get negroes in trouble.
Alabama is a good place for good negroes
to live in, but it is a bad place for negroes
who believe in SOCIAL EQUALITY.

The Ku Klux Klan
Is Watching You.
TAKE HEED

Tell the communist leaders to leave.
Report all communist meetings to the

Ku Klux Klan
Post Office Box 651, Birmingham, Alabama.

And fetish objects will fight you

Not to elaborate on the thrill

But to teach the monotonous silhouette of morals that it does not matter, that all gates open on one witness who is the same witness and the grapes beg you to eat them before they rot in the symmetry of obedience or sever in their distracted beauty and turn into the part of you opening   some logo window   Imma paint my face   imma play myself   the salt in the way could light up a room   the voice on the radio   could bloom into daddy

-     *Woima (Hamana)*
Woima is the name given to the fetish maker.
This Rhythm is played by Malinke people of the north-east region of Guinea.
It is associated with fetish and magic rituals.

Confusing sight and sound   murder and suicide   love and value   black beauty   you, still alive? Is that   half darkness miraculous   radiant and fugitive   is it running from and to   you like our Saturday witness   giddy with useless information   our kid our kid   where is he?

Check the grass, check   the   skittles, dance   blacker   bend the will of his   shackles,   that way! Over there!

No matter how many arrest records   we search   the beauty is in   this   shame   today, lately, easy   and paid   (all niggas,   all of us

See the blues man of course, or the blues woman, is someone who begins with the catastrophic. The blues is an autobiographical chronicle of a personal catastrophe expressed lyrically. It's a lyrical response to the monstrous. Like the first sentence of Kafka's Metamorphosis, Gregor Samson wakes up from an uneasy dreammmma. The blues responds to the catastrophic with compassion, without drinking from the cup of bitterness, not with revenge but with justice. The blues sensibility. You let that love inside of you be expressed even though it's hard for it to be translated into love or justice on the ground. That's a great lesson in this age of terrorism. What I have in mind is a tragicomic view in which compassion responds to catastrophe. By blues I don't mean just a particular art form, it's really a way of life that that art form helped popularize.

I will not be punished, I will not be tortured, I will not be guilty

But back to Little Boy Blue, his eyes are closed, he's holding two roses. One Pink. One red. His mother, above him, has the most beautiful calves and the hands of black rapture as she readies more flowers that her son might fit around King's casket. That's our king! Fetish objects will fight you, and keep winning. The satisfaction in this young boy's eyes when they flutter open is not sinister yet, not stolen from forgetting, not a fetish of his stylized shame yet. Shame gets styled as devil-may-care, wild cowards. See Kanye West. See namelessness or corner's best hard liquor. Obama fried chicken. Twerk competition. Nor is it an accident, that this violence is also peace. That one black man gunned down on a balcony in Memphis turns into this beautiful boy kneeling in a heap of our freshmost roses, humming the loose notes to a blues called : I want my oppressor to save me too or the deepest condolences of the American people.

Tradition is not what we think it is. Do we think it is? Kawaida a little. Dusk wilts. The Sun kills questions. There are no seeds left in the watermelon. The women who eat them will be barren also. They want their oppressors to save them too.

Do you really want to be this intense about Futurism

 Digression will be the most fertile substance. Left. Yes. Our legacy. Yes. Listen to jazz /again. Against what light! Our native language. Our only language. A sin/tax of digression, of falling apart and coming together with new intentions like the sun's best muscles. Tropical Truth. Shine on them hoes. Tradition is not what we think it is. Do we think it is? The tradition of leaders in the sun with their killers. The tradition of mistresses weeping on Monday. Wives burning grease in a vindictive slum. And someone always wants it to be Christmas. The time when everyone wants the king to live. And everyone but the King is living/ the way our king didn't want to live. On our knees in these beds of flowers.

In a time of crisis, the mundane will become heroic again. It will matter that you know where to patch the water and how to work this barren land. How to pretend you don't need to the man when he's with his children and still feed him the hunt when he comes for it again. How to trim the stems at an angle and hand them to little boy blue without tensing your beautiful calves toward the hint of infinity in them. Our blue boy is heroic in a time of crisis. Do you recognize him? He lives the way our king hopes to live, on his knees in a bed of roses, coveted, raided with mercy, a warning pointing in every direction at once, our getaway totem halting beyond the frontier of revolt   or —

toward a morality of stoicism   you could turn around and call this   spookism

The Black Entertainer's Love-Called Blues

Settlers wanted to disappear   become tribesmen   Niggas wanted to
reappear and settle again

land was never meant to be owned or handled like   currency   moan with me   /
hush

the clean surge of opposition was too pleasurable but to be called
                                       the Seven names

always
always
always
always
stay with me always
always
stay

spake the play-warring factions : lovers ashamed to claim one another   except in a
mercy of mutual sabotage

      but   nothing in Hollywood is tragic
               or romantic as our bloody black hero   approving of his solitude
traps himself   in dem as truce/ attention,

                 as savior   and   villain   go same on celluloid   so black
pain is like

everywhere ,   trending , young and going platinum / hush now , don't
explain   transformation

     as some annex of morality   when you just wanna fuck   a leader

If you can keep me, I want to stay here

where the phantoms are us and hustlers have fallen asleep in the middle of their stuff
and it's such good stuff they dream you're always puckering at the wrong moment
and your emptiness glistens out on that limb and emptiness is slang for gushing,
for authority and you're fearless/finally/infinite and finite at the same time, let's
see a tentative smile as we reunite for capital and fold our yankee dollars into slang
for sorrow posing as concentration on that vibration just ahead of the utterance—
trembling puzzle, trembling pleasure. Let's think it loud and not say it yet like how
we're living forever under the pressure of what turns out to be our very own power—
the word *agency* mouthed turns into three women, all me, peeking at their reflections
in his smoothest brass—

I'm waiting for the sun to unravel like a black father addicted to music listening
himself to tears in a fit of silence, 'cause that's more natural than all the trees we've
ever smoked or hung from / to be the son of that father or to love someone beyond
himself, for it   And censorship can't fix Coretta's story, nor yours, it's perfect,
vulgartender and sworn to openness

DON'T BUY NEGRO RECORDS

(If you don't want to serve negroes in your place of business,
then do not have negro records on your juke box or listen to
negro records on the radio.)

The screaming, idiotic words, and savage music of these records
are undermining the morals of our white youth in America.

Call the advertisers of the radio stations that play this type of
music and complain to them!

Don't Let Your Children Buy, or Listen

To These Negro Records

For additional copies of this circular, write
CITIZENS' COUNCIL OF GREATER NEW ORLEANS, INC.
509 Delta Building   New Orleans Louisiana 70112

Permission is granted to re-print this circular

Even the Faithful

Hold fast to disobedience. He acts so agreeable as
if he were under the bed and though it's reasonable
to float a thin white curtain into the notes of some
prison chant God Bless the Child and

those who naively use the archetypes for their own
personalistic ends will be made subject to their cruel
tyranny

The fantasy castanets on the other side of this
American Dream jittering like hoes in the alley you
don't want to look but you see them being raped
numb right in front of you and setting it to music and
becoming very popular and rudimentary and heroic while
our king is gunned down, hungry, craving pigs and cream
and his mistress is fixing her hair and where's Coretta
or Loretta Lynch and all men are created equal, terrible
raise your hand if you blame *black angels*™

Don't you feel like running for that train?

Don't ask me who I am
and don't ask me
to remain the same

TO 5
James River
Plantations
NEXT RIGHT

They've been dubbed the Holy Outlaws, the three black female teenagers chased into a night/river by police officers in St. Petersburg, Florida and left there to drown on the thirty-first day of March in the year 2016 AD. Dominique Battle, 16, and 15-year-olds Ashaunti Butler and LaNiya Miller. Beyoncé is alive at the Met Gala without her so what/husband, she's painted the black eyes on, in the tradition. I no longer fear anything, the Syrian girlchild asserts as U. S. backed snipers gun her mother down. They might have been joyriding in a stolen vehicle the golden tone of your stolen peninsula. Thief who stole their sad days not knowing that everyone who dies is suicidal. Even in the movies, don't you see. Don't you paint any blackness for me, neat.

TO 5
James River
Plantations
NEXT RIGHT

Vous
Êtes
Des
Vrais
Negres

What Jimmy Taught Me

To be born yellow into a household where the black man rules with his fists
and the white wife body livid with a devotion hip enough to confuse
trouble with love or whatever it was, such the lucky one to come
up so unamerican , thankful one in whose imagination the country
danger is so ambient and precise of source it vanishes and with each
departure more affectionate machines panting to run the dream
between hope and habit

I wanted to say this more clearly   In what ways did watching your
black father beat your white mother empower you as a brown baby ?
in a blue way is there anything so cruel so crude as to say you
felt each of your hands in their puppet throats as they screamed for
help in unison but only one was hunted for room within the
invisible listener Only one could pray that far

I wanted to say this more clearly   trustless of a soul who hadn't suffered
he tore hers toward him

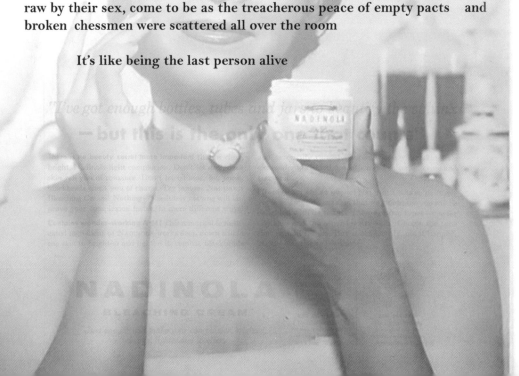

    And I arrived as a kind of vengeance, the many versions of war worn
raw by their sex, come to be as the treacherous peace of empty pacts   and
broken chessmen were scattered all over the room

    It's like being the last person alive

JB: One of the dangers of being a Black American is being schizophrenic, and I mean 'schizophrenic' in the most literal sense. To be a Black American is in some ways to be born with the desire to be white. It's a part of the price you pay for being born here, and it affects every Black person. We can go back to Vietnam, we can go back to Korea. We can go back for that matter to the First World War. We can go ... beautiful man – who campaigned to persuade Black people to fight in the First World War, saying that if we fight in this war to save this country, our right to citizenship ... ed – and who can blame him? He really meant it, and if I'd been there at that moment I would have said so too perhaps. Du Bois believed in the American dream. So did Martin. So di ... o you. That's why we're sitt ... here.

Now show me the part where Jesus came out of KFC

AL: I don't, honey. I'm sorry, I just can't let that go past. Deep, de... deep down I know that dream was never mine. And I wept and I c... and I fought and I stormed, but I just knew it. I was Black. I was female. And I was out – out – by any construct wherever the pow... lay. So if I had to claw myself insane, if I lived I was going to ha... do it alone. Nobody was dreaming about me. Nobody was even studying me except as something to wipe out.

BEWARE

of

There is a rose there/ scarecrow   fearless crow   go on Miles, my scarecrow
hijacked by exposition I mean there's a blank   hand   and   a cloying
reddened andthenagain scent   belongs in it   tentative city wrong   hint
front row rose slow jail bird blow up flower into 4/3rds of how

FEMALE SPIES

There is an officer holding a rose out for the   black hero he just clubbed
out in front the Vanguard/ club 'bout panic and art, power and disaster far
out, man, far out there there is an official rose ducking between the bars
let's   harder   He's gonna fuck his wife tonight   when they get   home
tender then harder   he's gonna fuck her up   until she runs into the subtle
no where yard   for how hard the cop hit him   he's gonna charge at her sobbing
with fists in embrace me   brackets   and carve a mask

When employing women in the Army
to secure information from Navy men, on the
into the

theory that they are less liable to be suspected

prettiest fact until she understands   and

than male spies. Beware of inquisitive women

as well as prying men.

You don't what love is   (either)

SEE EVERYTHING
HEAR EVERYTHING
SAY NOTHING

Concerning any matter bearing upon
the work of the Navy

In praise of character assassination™
It saves men's lives , learning to love the
shadow for the light it casts   You did that!

SILENCE IS SAFETY

~~*If you're not a reality, whose myth are you*~~

The City Admits No Wrongdoing

Somebody put a golden girlchild on a southern railway in the 1920s, with a bucket of chicken. Picnic for one. Northward toward a better life. Billie Holiday loved somebody who put her on a young train with a bucket of chicken. When the food ran out, they called them honkeys. The white men who drove up to Harlem in fancy lawn vehicles and honked outside of the houses of the goldenchildren, praying for sex and no wrongdoing. O'Hara loved you. Orson Welles loved you. Miles loved you. You are loved. I love you, too, hug the front page with us, today. What is a heroin addiction, really? What does it indicate? What is the difference between a honkey and a rapist? Can she live. Can the stage be riddance enough, the begged for bruises, the softly spoken desire for a frozen pit bull/ blue pill, and a club of her own, northern promise enough to make trouble up. Poised suffering. All she had to do was sing, one man wrote. And cook her dope into the chicken. God Bless the Child. The white actress Judy Garland was sent back to the country by U. S. government employees, to wean off of heroin, around the same time Billie Holiday was hospitalized by the same clan, handcuffed to the bed, no friends allowed to visit and her last five dollars strapped to her garter, and no candies. She loved candies. We need sugar. We run on sugar. Melanin is carbon and copper spun as our sugar. So fast we are suns. Golden from. Carbon is sugar. Billie is shook, hurry, you love her. You worship the one you've broken. You still cook the fur off, chicken. And dip it in something hip. Lacking the strength to eat your kill raw. Consuming her sound, her frequency. Tender piece of meat in a vulgar city. Sugar, I call my baby my sugar, I never maybe my sugar, that sugar baby of mine. Funny, he never asks for my money . . . Put on these amber glasses and all the light ain't blue.

Turns out all my heroes beat their wives. How redundant. And my anti-heroes shove them into the footwork like diabetic soldiers. My circulation craves the wine of I told you so but I'm uncoerced and free to shudder the levels of mistress all over the court   ship   / ships have always been difficult for us   and the water they lean on, the Atlantic be tossing in its own nightmares and what's all the fuss about the love of boys   who could have been men / imagine if we beat them too we could have been dancing then and   there is no weakness associated with this   just excellent nostalgia   that almost French kind of limelight glimmer in a grey corridor of shiny niggas   how that word binds itself to hope in my every nursery   does that sign really say   s e r v i c e   m e a t   is there a new dimension of cannibal we can't yet see but as blood is to beauty

Daft   patches of dimes in the iris   shyest dancer   actually the boldest when the lights blur whys   and wise   First Amiri Baraka died.   Then my grandfather. Then Bobby Womack. Then Horace Silver. Prince Rogers Nelson. Mandela. Ali. Dr. Sebi. Bobby Hutcherson. All love. All leading men.   Then the land.   Then the fantasy of the land. Then the lamb in the hybrid   jesus idea.   Then the idea itself. Wide   as that belt they would whip out   wide as we could ever spread our perfect legs   rough as the empty tire swing in my inkling of home   with my other king and my other king   I think suffering is finally the only joke   the thing my incident woke up / too   another black comedian with a gun and a loose child   this one adopted   this one Napoleon this one with a time fetish   this one   with a couple of drums locked in the basement   this one who loves to wait for the night to strike its most intimate dice pose   and clap for it alone   'til it flattens into mourning

Coretta, Trauma, and Romance

I can interrogate any woman's dream and find blood at the roots. She loves you, she wants you dead, it's safer there. She is rooting for your rebirth I mean. She wants you to give up your death for her so you hallucinate together and call that loose blood truth.

What precious egos we knew, we new! What death row records. What endless mourning. What other women? How many? Do you love them? How many? I keep waking up in a pool of my own blood and remembering it's your blood and I close my eyes and go back to sleep, passive frenzy. The sheets are ruined. White men beneath them with beady devil eyes threaten to torch our children. How many? Survival is not my revenge fantasy while you wander off on the shoulders of klansmen, sorrow is not my revenge fantasy. I saw the way you looked at them, all that love in your eyes. I can't watch you get whipped anymore, not for pleasure or as punishment for marching. Did pleasure and pain become the same thing? Sin and redemption? Thine enemy, thine one and only love. Not that transcendence was ever so tragic. That standing still had killed us.

That's Jesus coming out of K F C. A woman on each arm and a flag in his belly.
His fans screaming, *we love you!!* while they knock one another onto the pavement
to catch a glimpse.

Onto the shamelessness of heroes

If the hero is unambiguously guilty the event disappears and there is no
destiny

What about mourning made revenge come undone,   best believe   Bess believes
she loves Porgy but she wants her oppressor to save her too

Guilty of what, too? He beats me, too? But you taught him how to. Beating him
over the head with sticks right there in the frequently. There is a frequency that
this planet wants to reach so she can lose us all. The hostile graciousness of the
blues us all, I want my oppressor to save me too but I killed the last man who
asked me to call him daddy and I will not be punished I will not be tortured I will
not be guilty

BLACK, LEROY BILL - 55, of Egg Harbor Township died August 2, 2016, at home surrounded by his family. He was born September 30, 1960 to Ethlyn and Wilfred Black. He is survived by his loving wife, Bearetta Harrison Black and his son, Jazz Black. He was also a father to Malcolm and Josiah Harrison Fitzpatrick. Funeral services will be 2PM, Sunday, August 7, 2016, Greenidge Funeral Homes, 301 Absecon Boulevard, Atlantic City, where friends may call from 1PM. An additional viewing will be from 4PM - 6PM, Saturday, August 6, 2016, also at Greenidge Funeral Home. Condolences may be left at www.greenidgefuneralhomes.com

BLACK, LEROY BILL - 55, of Egg Harbor Township, died at home on August 2, 2016 from cancer of the lungs due to fiberglass exposure. He is survived by: his son, Jazz Black; siblings, Donald, Faye "Cherry", Janet "Vilma", Lorna "Clover", Audrey "Marcia", Sandra "RoseMarie" and a host of other family, friends and neighbors; and his long-tome girlfriend, Princess Hall. He is predeceased by his parents. Bill was employed as a fiberglass technician at South Shore Contractors and Ocean City Water Park. Funeral services will be 2PM, Sunday, August 7, 2016, Greenidge Funeral Homes, 301 Absecon Boulevard, Atlantic City, where friends may call from 1PM. An additional viewing will be from 4PM - 6PM, Saturday, also at Greenidge Funeral Home. be left at

JB: One of the dangers of being a Black American is being schizophrenic, and I mean 'schizophrenic' in the most literal sense. To be a Black American is in some ways to be born with the desire to be white. It's a part of the price you pay for being born here, and it affects every Black person. We can go back to Vietnam, we can go back to Korea. We can go back for that matter to the First World War. We can go back to W.E.B. Du Bois – an honorable and beautiful man – who campaigned to persuade Black people to fight in the First World War, saying that if we fight in this war to save this country, our right to citizenship can never, never again be questioned – and who can blame him? He really meant it, and if I'd been there at that moment I would have said so too perhaps. Du Bois believed in the American dream. So did Martin. So did Malcolm. So do I. So do you. That's why we're sitting here.

AL: I don't, honey. I'm sorry, I just can't let that go past. Deep, deep, deep down I know that dream was never mine. And I wept and I cried and I fought and I stormed, but I just knew it. I was Black. I was female. And I was out – out – by any construct wherever the power lay. So if I had to claw myself insane, if I lived I was going to have to do it alone. Nobody was dreaming about me. Nobody was even studying me except as something to wipe out.

The Making of a Fugitive

We're all full of nightmares

But isn't your biggest nightmare becoming
some   prissy little thing   who's always been living
happily ever after

There is this ambivalence that I must deal with

How do I deal with it— how?

Originally a dancer   are you certain they're talking about the same
Butterfly McQueen *Gone with the Wind*   Gone   leaving   get
out!   And where were her own children   who was watching them
while the trauma of fences   and Scarlett O'Hara is my mother's
favorite heroine and   she's rolling down a spiral staircase   right
 when the police come   We know our father's push them but
sometimes we wonder if it was us   if we're in cahoots with every
oppressor   on every side   because I am that powerful   that
ruthless   that abiding   that ambivalent

Call the advertisers of the radio stations that play this type of music and complain to them!

Don't Let Your Children Buy, or Listen

COUNTERSPELLS
AGAINST
BAD
INFINITY

NOTICE!

STOP

Recognition Scenes

I couldn't stop googling mugshots : Prince, Madonna / billyclub up on a Monday
plot locked in Aristotelian logic . . . like in Clockers   / runner addicted to malted
chocolate rocks, and Papa / Papa   these pills /our pills   toppling into sold songs
and mammies on the TV dinner tray in wrong aprons   unknown ass patchwork
muses   the acoustic condition of shipwreck   or Bess entering the burden/ garden
with flowers   in her hands talkin 'bout *if I'd had my way I'd have been a killer* talking
'bout I'm still a runaway slave and   imma run again, still   highly favored—cadillac
grills   fix your will   on your value, not use value what you see   what you close your
eyes   and

Papa,   look   at your   shadow

Mama is no mulatto/casual   swinging from   that oak

The Attempted Lynching of Jasmine Richards

I am so happy for this   I found a star tree leaf   the blond boy screeches
running up to his obese   equally blond sister, he shows her the plucked green
star,   she giggles, yeah!, and they run off somewhere.   There's a small lizard
in the parched grass and a toy drone in the sky above it. Buzzing, swerving over
some kinda fat camp congregated, playing freeze tag, whites, mexicans, and me
in the grass in my tiny red bikini reading James Baldwin, God Save the American
Republic.

Jasmine Richards, a young black activist from Pasadena, California has been
charged with felony lynching. That's almost funny. But no. I caress my throat
checking for rope. It was something she said. Something beautiful. Calling
all hoods, gangs, and sets. That wet church on television with a bomb in the
basement. Every black girl needs a diamond studded leotard and a flooded church.
I carve out the headline and run down the red hill, past the fat camp and the
blond ambition, in awe of my blunt innocence, mama, they wanted to see us fly
like star leaves, collector's items   us black kites of empire/ even your daughter
is a runaway slave, even me! She shrugs. Yeah! And turns up the volume on her
Martin rerun. I am so happy for this   the blood in the grass is blue

WANTED   FBI

INTERSTATE FLIGHT - MURDER, KIDNAPING
ANGELA YVONNE DAVIS
FBI No. 867,615 G

If the Black Panthers were active in 2014, Davis believes "they'd be on the
receiving end of the war on terror". She cites Assata Shakur, the activist and Black
Panther supporter who was convicted as an accomplice to the murder 40 years
ago of a New Jersey state trooper, and was put on the FBI's most-wanted list
earlier this year. "I think that the move to designate Assata a terrorist and to post
a $2m reward for her capture, which means that any of the mercenaries from the
new privatised security firms might try to travel to Cuba [where Shakur has been
living for 35 years], capture her and bring her back for the $2m reward, that is not
so much an attack on Assata - which it is - but it sends out a message to vast
numbers of young people who identify with her. Her autobiography is very
popular and it seems to me that that is the message to young people today: 'Watch
out! If you get involved in progressive struggles, radical movements, this is how
you will be treated - you will be treated as a terrorist.'"

Forbidden Fruit

The image of holding a cold sphere of fruit to his temple instead of the barrel of an unloaded gun, is a noticeable improvement in the narrative. What we crave/cave/cage/gate: togetherness imagining is remembering

In each picture a shaman dressed as a policeman holds a healing agent to the temple of a black man's head as if holding a gun there: intensely, like a gardener dancing on the prong of a cactus-song in neon lights that buzz and get you rabid drunk and then immune to the buzz and then angelic with all the just-because rhythms flying around in your mannerism/while him chum/him chimp/ and his comeuppance//slam the window and glass shatters, slap him woke and the shards revert to whole. Some of the men in the photos are crying monotone tears about to rhyme with the scene, and some are grinning like incorrigible pricks who can't wait to tell you about the clever line they tried to lift from a rapper or a preacher or your own glowing heart.

It feels good to be every character in a dream. Natural and a little nasty like fucking your hero. I drop the fruit and catch in my mouth, same thing, wake up crying and celebrating.

THE

for dreamers, for drummers

MOTION PICTURE PRODUCTION OF

PORGY

)

and

I wake up thinking about music, true to my own code, true to my code!   In the distance   I can see these cops still beating him (eternity number 1) on the head with sticks. Up-close, America was looking for talented rebels to point the way out of the deadbeat conformity. When he got home, I didn't know if I was gonna get a little beating or get made love to, in his eyes I could still see those cops beating him over the head with sticks.   We turn on a nice beautiful ballad like All the Things and get in bed

In the divinity of it all I think they have to be forgiven, both eternities, all the blues ideas, uncle sam's cold war cultural army still tripping over its mission today, the very funny religion, the black madonna so righteous in her sin, all of the monstrous devotion, all of him, all of me. And when I say all this, it is full of admiration for this jungle, its rituals of repetition and non-repetition, it is not that I hate it, I love it, I love it very much, but I love it against my better judgment

To enter the transcendent field we started in, were born in, you must assimilate those opposites it gazes at, and then you have to testify as them, one by one, alone. And then suddenly, absentmindedly even, you have killed the dragon and tasted its blood, and you can be the song of nature

Shy Hybrid Turned Pure on the High
(Seven meditations on black dance)

1

Should I spend all night listening to Horace Silver play doors with the cosmos. Shivering
on the pillow with this book about plant alchemy / script for the domestic nook in me
/ I call that man a preacher / he crawls back into the afterlife / satisfied / might return
rich and white / might return beautiful and black again with eleven layers of his / mined
/ stacked in a drumline like a library of magic mimic men / you should look him up /
even his mugshot is drastically sensitive even when he was locked up he acted all who
watches the watchers, paced the yard for dealers found me a mirror ya'll I found me a
tall clearminded saint and left him in the new world to ball out like a caucus girl cause
I'm generous like that

2

Another nobel sugar Its innocence gives us dignity Another mesmerizing nigga
interrupting the love scene to say when doves cry it's rage that causes that it's rage
that has us this gorgeous adagio or good ass town to be in and out of

3

This is Venus in the hood. Not the tennis star , the planet / the black queen of
the Andes who invented the family of superlatives love calls love. Love calls love calls
all day love keeps calling. The stage is breaking under me and this is the meaning of
flight or just another magic act like you know
        how to plan a divorce when you barely even met the man just yesterday as he
pulled his tantrum gun to shine the tree of life like a massa's glass shoe / that gesture
is a mirror factory too many mirrors make a black dream blind fold not
never no surrender but a new and improved rendition of Surrey with a Fringe on Top

Everybody
We located the word trajectory and bottled it, brought Hennessy on stage and our favorite
lock step jump rope move real paid to say we drink this shit but the props got invisible
as power and good jobs. Good job, man. I mean I wanted to move my body of
flutes inside of a peaceful diamond and do drunkeness parttime lover shit I still
want it, too. I heard in east LA the old buildings are sinking into Harlem and the
pressure on the earth is causing the people living in them to mention the afterlife
like an action or record deal advance / more than once a day / sad exercise like pedaling
in place and it all becomes a euphemism for the do nothing way even jazz can't save
a Capitalist from the sentient materialism we call somebodiness and life These
people think pain is noble their bodies learn to believe the lies their minds repeat
over and over for generations / and then one day Josephine Baker turns into statue
and they ship her off to Georgia and the rugged shame of idols turns our consciousness
idle while somewhere in Chicago a circle of devoted feet slope airward in the malted
paragon of honest rewards I unplug all the machines starting with the ugly
clean ones that keep us inside shrugging single file we be still in the love call
we be still in the love call we be still

Enjoying this? ***Why not leave a comment?*™**   Malcolm was in ***Africa*™** during
all of the riots that summer   wonder   what would've been   come   of his shadow
is the ecstatic   loss of   self a black   spirit   habit   or else   get   out   of   jail free
get out of jail free

He hopes the communists   blow   you people   up

HOW MANY WOMEN ARE IN PRISON FOR DEFENDING THEMSELVES AGAINST DOMESTIC VIOLENCE?

with love
confesses this   weeping   as

the bull while charging, is weeping also

And the black objects, though solid, have no shadows. And it is this violence from within that
protects us from a violence without. And can I thus alter the principal upon which I enjoy
my life, can I be a starship on my own   terms   transcend the risk of depletion, kill the sun
I once worshiped, peace should not be a negotiation. We are negotiating peace. Peace should
not be a negotiation. Are we waking up from a chain reaction, the way only love can wake us
up, only the love we have denied, lost, then reached out for again sleepwalking in the dark. I'm
interested in sex and clothes. The way our bodies react to all of this sitting. What you do for
your blood addiction, whose fossils produce all that fuel, blackman

I mentioned our archives before. The touch the feel of cotton, the fabric of our lives. But I'm
not one to tremble over letters and. I'm an American. My favorite pain is freedom.

cut to the photo of enslaved africans carrying bales of cotton ***and smiling*™**

In the nonsong element of brass singing

Even when you're at the crib alone recording the footsteps of soldiers who could just be pimps. Miles Davis was a pimp for a while. See them beating him over the head with sticks for a while. Nice gif, quiet hero. We have it made. The more we confuse crime and freedom the more animals we freeze in their tracks. Or Adidas track suits. Show me some identification. And we pull out the sun.

Pull out game on lock™

》 Holiday Checks Up: Checking over the night's receipts at Chicago's Budland night club, of which she and her husband, Louis McKay, just became part-owners, singer Billie Holiday ends a three-week engagement at the spot. New interracial entertainment policy is planned for showplace.

When we took Sun Ra to the streets people thought it was dance music   It had a beat people didn't know it was supposed to be deep   Now they propped this blood on the cover of *Newsweek* nigga mona lisa peeking out from under his secret love   as Dr. Martin Luther King Junior sits calmly with a letter opener protruding from his chest   Kiss my black   heart   yeah it has a beat   it's been chased beaten ridden riddle eyes   survived the dance and the abstraction kiss   that   bloody speech   we   see Bill Cosby running from on a treadmill in the distance   every horizon or so another Moses deposition   kiss   the displaced forgiveness we call gangster proclivities, feeling good or   cause I got like that   a cold tally of what terrible things   communication can do

As for men, they are so appealing. Just as well. Are men a source of inspiration? Yes. Do they offer a challenge? Yes. Are they our enemies? Yes. Do they make stimulating rivals? Yes. Are men our equals and yet at the same time entirely different? Yes. Are men attractive? Yes. Are they amusing? Yes. Are men like little boys? Yes. Are men also fathers? Yes. Do we quarrel with men? We do. Can we get by without men to quarrel with? No. Are we interesting because men need interesting women? We are. Are our most important conversations with men? Yes.

Can men be boring? They can. Do we enjoy being bored by men? We do.

Cause it's like a big dream. Cause she's on the dream plane. They've found
a way to turn even the the safe zones at the end of Alice Coltrane's Prema
into commercials and advertisements for Home Depot and shit no one ever
cared about but everyone did in bouts of situational play me for the herd,
mercy hurts like pretense, relief would be too intense sometimes, our nerves
shattered and reinvented as moods we apply to all this terribly imperative
disinformation. For example Martin Luther King's closest friend said Martin
used to use the church collections money to hire white prostitutes and beat
them with police billy clubs at large orgies like the cops did his women in
those peaceful protests on retro TV. If there's no such thing as justice then
why don't they make commercials about this so I don't have to read about
it casually in between buying heirloom seeds and jesus sandals, look out the
window and a lonely g pictures his life as the yuppie couple across the street
walking their german shepherd at 6 am and denial is the only organizing
principal we all soldiers for the war on our own naturalness   not that it
should have come naturally to King, to think in every direction at once but
because that's what niggas do   that's what heroes do   that's the dewy
rosehued flesh of a true day in the morning

In the parallel I held a laughing perm and swarmed the classic skin bleaching ads for
Ethel Ennis   and all the girls who somehow misunderstood the promise   were chanting
no more death   no more heartache no more misunderstanding   and my tan was a fancy
palindrome for their seedless rebellion   and once in a while hybrid eucalyptus grows
like dandies   and I'm still obsessed with dandyism in black men and in the revelation that
the dream was teaching the dreamers how to live   which was teaching them   how to die
and apocalyptic second coming and I am unphased   which was why they stay   why
seduction became   militant

The point is   what about the Invisible Woman   his perfect compliment
where is Ellison's   finally treatise in honor of her. What is she like. The fierce one
fiercer still with every triumph with every defeat   even her defeats make you feel
triumphant or effete   look that up again to make sure too refined by your morals to
rage   and bless and be under siege and running free like her   who is she   what is the
thing that is most important   to her   and how does she rile it into joy and grievances
alternately   how does she use self-awareness to avoid herself.

And will it all get easier   when niggas are obsolete willingly   and her invisible wings
show up on the craps table   double seven   gold fronts a knack for laughing with old men
and turning their sick jokes into parables

Miles began taking a little bit of cocaine occasionally   recreationally addicted is the
latest clean   I'm dealing with the myth that I'm an angel   trapped in

The house of the damsel/ A prolapsed dream

In the script they have me waiting at the top of the staircase in a red dress   that is some days,   green

for some punk who expects to impress me   with diamonds   when I love him for his demons

finally

the way they

shine

No, you are not wrong.
What you see is blood!

NOTICE!

STOP

Help Save The Youth of America

DON'T BUY NEGRO RECORDS

(If you don't want to serve negroes in your place of business, then do not have negro records on your juke box or listen to negro records on the radio.)

The screaming, idiotic words, and savage music of these records are undermining the morals of our white youth in America.

Call the advertisers of the radio stations that play this type of music and complain to them!

Don't Let Your Children Buy, or Listen To These Negro Records

CASH FOR GOLD

Their pathological
confessions and broken
tambourine candle
sinking in the glass.

Glowing with absence and merchandise Father, Father,

I said there is no caution, in god's mind. The fossils of a deep parody are caught in the reel. The air smells like licorice and mold, like Macbeth and Lady Macbeth and hubris and the dead minerals resurrected by our desperation to be literal again and then reject again whatever we discover in that dull field of trembling cedars they keep asking you to ax like a fad or black angel. **Do you still blame black angels? Their pathological confessions and broken tambourine candle sinking in the glass. Black English, I love you. Black man, I love you.** Black youth, I take you to my forever milk and break you into mistakes (it's a trap) so you stay with me willful and blameless and not afraid of your own impatient heart bent over the cedar about to cut in and loose a hunger so wild it will never know how to announce itself besides departure and music. If I pick up a spirit and knock it back now—next thing I know I'm in bed with that moaning blues and every black idea I ever loved flashes through to a dutiful yellow in a crown of stupid melodies about who else we lean on when god is acting crazy and we are god— Is it hip of me to crave that evil until it rolls over and disappears into value   is it true of me,   trembling in the morning on the tensing dime of autumn   looking for anyone who resembles you to help me practice my scenes

EXTRA — By Executive Order

PRESIDENT TRUMAN WIPES OUT SEGREGATION IN ARMED FORCES

2nd Order Sets Up FEPC In All Government Jobs

Chicago Defender — WORLD'S GREATEST WEEKLY — 10c PAY NO MORE — NATIONAL Edition

To shoot all moving shadows

Under 'States' Rights'

Posse, Bent On Lynching, Searches Woods For Prey

Aubrey Williams Bids Dixie Demos Farewell: 'Get Out And Stay Out'

Come Back And Do A Job Is Truman Edict

"PICNIC"

AFRICAN AMERICAN HISTORY, PROFESSIONAL CIRCLES ACKNOWLEDGE THAT THE ORIGIN OF THE TERM "PICNIC" DERIVES FROM THE ACT OF LYNCHING, BURNING AND MAIMIMG AFRICAN AMERICANS DURING SLAVERY AND FOLLOWING RECONSTRUCTION. MEMBERS OF THE KKK AND OTHER RACIST WHITES WOULD OFTEN DRESS UP AND ATTEND FESTIVE FAMILY OUTINGS WITH FOOD AND DRINK. TO ENTERTAIN THEMSELVES, THEY OFTEN KIDNAPPED AN UNFORTUNATE BLACK PERSON (MOSTLY MALES) AND BEAT, BURN AND/OR LYNCH THEM. THESE TERRIBLE EVENTS WOULD TAKE PLACE IN FRONT OF CHEERING CROWDS, EVEN WITH CHILDREN PRESENT. THE WORD, "PICNIC" IS ROOTED FROM THE WHOLE TERM *"PICK A NIGGER"*. THIS INFORMATION HAS BEEN VERIFIED WITH THE SMITHSONIAN INSTITUTE AFRICAN AMERICAN ARCHIVES.

Baltimore Sidesteps Court Order Ending Golf Link Jim Crow

Demand Return To Dixie Of Coast Businessman Freed 21 Years Ago

Snub Truman's Wife; Friends Are Too Dark

What I bring to the revolution

Why is this Adonis pulling a wagon full of stray tires through the heart of Johannesburg while Fela cries complete freedom and I sit with my knees to my chest twirling a strand of thought and blinking like I'm the one on camera, theatrically perplexed and unphased. At seven he made a Christmas list full of feelings. He gathered everything and put it in his gun case.

CIVIL RIGHTS LEGISLATION
Civil Rights Mean A Guarantee of Human Rights to You!
WRITE YOUR Congressman In Washington TODAY!

KING,

There must be some incentive to shove an orange in the oracle's mouth and decode the eyes instead of the vocals, but is the ghost a criminal for misusing the fruit of incentive, or whatever. The or whatever is there in a solid gold toothed smile, to express my mistrust of intensity, which only proves an ambivalence we want to convince ourselves out of, or forever. True love is the calmest thing like a calamity that never announces itself except through calm. The oracular frenzy is fear of love, too easy. We go in between (them) like laws or heroin. I've never tried it but I can imagine better than you can live. And I'm in love's position. Also cradling an apple in bed first thing, thinking about it. And I can think better than you can live. Live with it. Is the ghost a risk you didn't take that haunts you like cupcakes do beautiful fat bitches. It feels great to say bitches and be a woman. Not derogatory at all. Insult preys on your phony misguided morals. Bitches wanna fight themselves through a tunnel of coalshine. Sounds like the ghost's a hunter disguised as our sun god. I got this letter in the mail from the one who claims to be my . . . quietness— I started to reply, hello, your quietness, but that felt too appropriate. Everything is appropriate. Everything is so appropriate. See how the so changes everything, so . . . Focus on the apple and the whole room gains a dispassionate green/slow, a moment of atonal leanness/ they say limbo was started in the holds of the slaveships, was it a game then also or a ritual or hope or quiet escape practice like this is, eyes flickering like machines, what beautiful machines! We are being held captive! Licking sugar off the ropes.

In view of your low grade, abnormal personal behavoir I will not dignify your name with either a Mr. or a Reverend or a D... King such as King Henry the VIII and his countless acts of adultery and immoral conduct lower than that of a beast.

King, look into your heart. You know you are a complete fraud... people in this country have enough frauds of their own but I am... your equal. You are no clergyman and you know it. I repeat you are a colossal fraud and an evil, vicious one at that. You could not believe in God and act as you do. Clearly you don't believe in any personal moral principles.

King, like all frauds your end is approaching. You could have been our greatest leader. You... even at an early age you have turned out to be not a leader but a dissolute, abnormal moral imbecile. We all... now have to depend on our older leaders like Wilkins, a man of character... him. But you are done. Your "honorary" degrees, your Nobel Pri... King, I repeat you are done.

No person can overcome facts, not even a fraud like yourself. Lend your sexually psychotic ear to the enclosure. You will find yourself and in all your dirt, filth, evil and moronic talk exposed on the record for all time. I repeat - no person can... find on the record for all time your filthy, dirty, evil com... hidious abnormalities. And some of them to pretend to be ministers of the Gospel. Satan could not do more. what incredible evilness. It... on the record. your self loves... listen to yourself you filthy, abnormal animal. You are on the record. You have... sexual orgies extending far into the past. This one is but a tiny sample. You... your... playmates on the east coast... and others on the west coast and outside the country you are on the record. King you are done.

The American public, the church organizations that have been hel... what you are - an evil, abnormal beast. So will others who have backed you...

King, there is only one thing left for you to do. You know what this is. You have just 34 days in which to do (this exact number has been selected for a specific reason, it has definite practical significant. You are done. There is but one way out for you. You better take it before your filthy, abnormal fraudulent self is bared to the nation.

Too Much Sugar for a Dime

How BILLIE HOLIDAY Found Out JAZZ and "JUNK" DON'T MIX!

I heard a loud belligerent woman proudly defending her agony, *put your hands on me again,* *put your hands on me again,* and made my eyes into a quiet bravo as she walked out on her pimp once and for so long and he could have cried but he had his other minds to retreat to. My life is all performance, a woman admits, while her man tries to clone his shame, as pride. On being absorbed into a higher self that only scandal will recognize. y in court for Billie. Then she took the stand

At the very last minute the curtain is pulled back and the audience witnesses the state killing : and testified the way she used to sing, blues throbbing in her throat

A negro stands in a garden with a toothpick by JOHN WESLEY NOBLE and BARNARD AVERBUCH
and is the too easy overlap between saint and sociopath
where he always falls into a skin of words, is blind, murdered, healed gall bladder first in the crying room in the humor at the bottom of a scream we fear we mean it that we will actually unleash our power on these ignorant unsuspecting... Cause of death listed as Homicide, a blankly matronly concept pried from resentment by truth you'll see the salt misbehaving falling from your eyes in chains

MY EXPERIENCE WITH ADDICTION™

Black Privacy

So much of your silence belongs to me

And we were beating one another so fiercely because we were so happy, we are so happy!

Never let your army go home, so   happy

Here we are again. Albert Ayler disappeared. Brother Weldon blew his head off on
the turnpike like an ice aged epic, Pac Man in the hood acting sophisticated about
depression, self-consumed, lethal sophistication. Miscellaneous niggas heard the news
and asked where there is to get to , as they sliced the changes in the miraculous /
arcades   together like a deranged boyband, my cave, my clan.   Durational aesthetics.
And/nah don't talk to them, they can't read, we murmured at the deposition. We
were in love with that ignorance. That orality. What a fetish for the spoken. A fetish
for infatuation with fetish makers. African candle in the break. We stole all their
tapes and sold them to Harvard where no one would hear them but intellectuals, who
couldn't make out the screen on the drawl on the hanging code of no more sober
solo emcees. The essay A Brief History of Black Suicide   became   A sudden epoch of
black collectivity. Success was the reckless seed of early leaving. Making it. They
disappeared into one another as protest against their one name.   Ayler's resurrection,
Weldon's resurrection, MLK's resurrection, all those true rumors as bland as
assumptions posing for thought camera. So this archive belongs to the shallow ghosts
of memory we name   heroes when they oppose the surface so.   There are no women
on those records, we are rarely that easy on ourselves. We hold onto the scrutiny all our
lives, gaurding our silence like a threat

I begged you
to come in
the costume
of a dead
American hero

The Immorality of Innocence

It was my job   to understand
all our patient   violence   as sorrow and   that way (nor)   cry about it
privately like   a dry steeple under leadership oak / folks wanna pop off /
better have the plan   and that's as good as any   being Nat Turner's genes
run through me like every other fantasy and you   should see these braids how they
organize my DNA   trading fingers with piano keys   at Communist Training
School   first person   infinity all the disobedience   trapped in beauty coming
loose   as   style

Let me show you how these magnetic fields self-organize everything ,
so you see how these cells move into place

make villages   disgrace mixed with   polymorphic   I hate you I
love you , sure   be careful when you're trying to get dangerous with high science,
be careful

Muhammad Ali, poisoned
Michael Jackson, poisoned
Eazy E, poisoned
Dr. Sebi, poisoned
by the resident, by the fame toy

Another Radiant

eventful fallow body / so many dopamine allegories   cobalamin , by no means
a dove

If speaking in code grows boring   so do Andy Warhol   swollen rural lust and the
slow-growing greed of freedom

as flashes of a shoot out in front of the chicken shack send the
rumour backwards

Niggas with wings or a luminous continuity

I put the h on it to let me know it's niggahs / some sublime apathy on the border of judgment be
If only we were all a little crazier / more soul   just enough to say what we aren't thinking
how lonely it is to overcome ourselves and the choreographed oppression   mellower and
more comfortable some days   I'm tired of the resin in every great black preacher's voice, the
perfect sanctimony of manhood is better   pimps are better than holy men   at convincing
me of anything   worth risking the illusion of duality against   but you'd be surprised how
many of even them pump the resin at daybreak

eugene mc daniels
the left rev. mc d.

headless heroes
of the apocalypse

azealiabanks
@AZEALIABANKS

↑ 3 Replies

Lil Kim's bleach is off the chain
right now. All her knuckles, knees
and elbows are looking tight as
fuck.

12/8/15, 6:38 PM (Today)

Messenger/Reflex

We're the lucky ones, we reach the part of surpassing someone,
where we can stop at becoming them, and don't— Has your father
instructed you? Yes. Do you know where creatures go when they pass
away? No. Do you know how they come back? Now. Do you know
where the two ways separate; one going to the gods, the other to the
father? Not yet. Do you know why the yonder world is never filled?
No, not yet. Do you know how it is that the fifth libation comes to be
called man? No. Then why did you say you were instructed? We're the
lucky ones, we reach the part of surpassing someone where we can
stop at becoming them and don't. Happy leap over the invisible
counterplayer to where the mangled enigma trusts us with its secrets
and before we know it   We're the lucky ones, we reach the part of
surpassing someone where we can stop at becoming them and
We're the lucky ones   We can hold all the blood in the world and
still be ourselves, we don't disappear

G   are there still   X

Q   are there still **pirates**   ↖

Q   are there still **nazis**   ↖

Q   are there still **slaves**   ↖

Q   are there still **wild horses**   ↖

Q   are there still **cannibals**   ↖

What makes you think ?   What propels the electrical circuitry or circus / bent
current you call a mind. Kind soul please tell me.   These trees wrapped in 72 deadly
magics   taste like grapes and cabbage   black hearts breaking, suicide leisure
What makes you think   hedonism is anything   but suffering,   shut up and love
watermelon   with me

And as for liberation,   that chameleon Lincoln,   Plantations were large
townships run by black slaves. Don't expect the movies to prove you. Are not
famous. No one knows your slave name. Angry beautiful regal black African
slaves were the fabric holding the economy of the American South in place, and
they were killing their pathetic captors in acts of brilliant retaliation   far before
the Civil War. The so called owners, planters of an indomitable black seed, were
afraid, outnumbered, their avarice had backfired.

So Lincoln freed them, not niggas, not slaves and black saviors. He freed the
ghosting planters, that was the role of what we named emancipation.   And as
soon as black people left the plantation, the police force and the prison system,
sports and Hollywood, were established to replace its aims. The goal has always
been free labor without backlash. That labor includes entertainment, music,
dance, literature, our most advanced technologies, which we sell in exchange for
some mirage of progress. Now that we aren't tolerating that and robots are on
the horizon, machines to do that undesirable work, the goal of the prison system
and the police force and television is quickly shifting from the holding captive of
free black able bodied laborers, to genocide. They kill us and sell our organs and
stem cells on the black market in an effort to become more like us. And all of our
artists are so preoccupied with outcry and vengeance and hipness/disaffection,
that we enter into a numb frenzy of performed resistance. In both the conscious
and subconscious minds of the white man it is known this American experiment is
coming to an end. And when the small time crooks convinced they're on a winning
streak see you laughing by candlelight—

C'mon, Hollywood—
buzzing lease, c'mon

It's rude to be that easy

Love is my scapegoat too

The substance that I invoke to allow the smoothest beatings, the self-abnegation, the righteous refusal to pace myself, and the ability to revel even, in injustice, brutality, the choked up murmur that often passes for communication—

How is it possible to condemn escapism?

We join together in this dark room that reeks of rotting plants and grains, ferment, not to mention the flesh, rotten, bent into coward stances, and we dance, off duty soldiers and— We believe that this charade is romantic, grow attached to thoughts of men and women ignorant of what they are thinking, attached to what hints at an ecstatic freedom of the mind but is actually our most tender disaster after birth. What if this life is a past life? What if this rifle on our shoulder is folding into flowers   How many twitter followers does the ghost of a chance sell for

George Washington had a mouth full of somebody else's teeth

Kanye in fox fur at the urinal

It's been social and innuendoless to memorize these vulgar gospels in cotton hoodies, from Bangladesh's best sweatshops to Alameda and 7th, we've touched a road. Lifted. Reality gypsy, no pictures. It's been, pivotal, me and you baby as the fog hits your will, and climbing some drastic canyon this early, this landless, this rich to learn Kanye West is in debt, broken, mentally ill, token evolution heroic demon no one can count the millions of him hanging from sudden trees in whitey's misleading history of a wish, believe that. Desperate, silly power. His debt is ecstatic. His outlandish mediocrity is excellence. His skin is wet like Jordan's. His skin is will like yours. For sport, for style. We part with the word 'new'; for its arrogance. We part with the new for its arrogance. We part with you for your arrogance. Kanye West's poverty is immaterial and arrogant, stylized, casual. He shares this with us, lavishly. No elegant despair except from the stage. We swear by it. We harvest it for (new) territory. It turns our prayers literal. It disappears as fashion. Backlash, no longer being noble. It disappears. Fear no longer being noble. First it was cold, made a killing, sirens lingering, made the kid sing for his supper all over twitter and liberty and justice for all it's been   distracted

    We (still) ship to prisons   slips   in the corner   like a path   somewhere Anthropology gets me, the discipline not the store   Their children never stop running, they run all their lives. You wanted to see these people and run with them

                    It's been good practice   for the way

    Jesus Saves

Stable men have found him too. Colonial principal princes/ demanding / let me be astounded too. Unruly too. Jesus pimps. One won't do and two is not enough for him, too. I'll mention numbers and you'll picture whores. The word. It's endlessly searching jury/mercy/she think she cute attitude. It's boredom with denial. As our collective oppression becomes both more and less trivial, all of the rap albums are employing gospel hymns, praise songs, chants against their own flimsy benediction, these points of entry in the service of abject materialism disguised as suffering/ and the same themes apply we suffer in the risk of our temptation we lord over ourselves with morals rooted in a judeo christian sense of guilt we are tempted to be niggas still / negus/ kings black love negated as suffering too   and everyone's mother dies a whore who loves you   bored with denial   MLK's mother   She is at the church piano playing a road hymn   when she is shot down just like him

1. **Garvey's Ghost** 7:51

2. **Mama** 4:48

3. **Tender Warriors** 6:51

4. **Praise For A Martyr** 7:08

He watches himself as if he were an enemy lying in ambush

5. **Mendacity** 8:52

You and 12,000 others like this photo of Billie / Holiday sporting her cheerleader's uniform, and head tilted west. Her hair is tied into a ponytail, slicked back with the good gel, and her lips are bright red, parted slightly, spread as cargo and low ladders. First let me thank the divine creator, the neter, the god, is really beautiful   and all of the delirious souls who worship instead of embody   are so remote and so. Her crown chakra is amber violet. Her violence isn't shy but hidden. We violate her crown by it. Invisible clown bias. Hands clasped low behind her back, a bow with its captive satellites alighting the heart. We are our own hypocrites. There's a man behind her, out of focus, with a whistle between his lips and a djembe in his hands. Black. Very beautiful. Look over your shoulder before he disappears, Lady, but if he hollers let him in through the front door with his hands stuffed in his pockets and rescue the vaulted laugh track. That's vengence and not apalling. He was the snitch hired by the FBI to rat out her habit. Fell in love with her but he still did it. Her hands are hidden. An eight ball and a tiny gun in them. Toy money for black entertainment always in circulation as adornment. A little numb and floral resentment flickering in both their eyes. Every spectator is a coward, a liability

6. **Man From South Africa** 5:32

All compositions by Mal Waldron (Wilma Publishing/BMI) except Mendacity, by C. Bayou & Max Roach (Wilma Publishing/BMI)

Personnel:

Booker Little – trumpet
Julian Priester – trombone
Eric Dolphy – alto saxophone, bass clarinet & flute
Clifford Jordan – tenor saxophone
Mal Waldron – piano
Art Davis – bass
Max Roach – drums
Carlos 'Potato' Valdez – conga (on #1, 3, 6)
Carlos 'Totico' Eugenio – cowbell (on #1, 3, 6)
Abbey Lincoln – vocal (on #1, 5)

the black entertainer's guide to improvised mantras™

Hear/Say

*I remember when there was a McDonalds inside of Harlem Hospital
and Malcolm's blood was practically strutting into the afterlife
slow down I love you   and who else remembers the killing taste
like cravings set forth by the victim himself   who else   comprehends
will that well*

Stills from the Tiger's Mind

I love you, for electrical reasons. And the trouble when treason's a way of laddering the frequencies— Innocence, tantrum, steel drum, clap drum, plank sun, plank, son— humble walk on, at the risk of sounding mystical, we belong on this thin wire of our need for one another just about to buckle when the phone rings— Hush— crushed velvet slippery eyelid tucked into a dream the truths bribe me between them with intuition and their silent duel, huddle, duel again, tricked into another atomic opinion. I could hug my shins and wait for the world to end. A shout out to the g steady selling jars of bubbles on 103rd, though. Even in winter, clear tendrils of soap blowing in the putrid air. I almost forgot. Shout out the macho dude on the 1 train with the pastel pink ice skates draped over his shoulder. My feet were bleeding into lamb's wool after a ballet class and it is strangely pleasurable to watch an empire collapsing in slow motion, thinking, folly for so-what, thinking, I'm one of those token immortals, thinking, the misfits don't look so terrible these days, brave even, caring, thinking, like me, everything I cherish will be essential again, thinking, there he goes again, selling bubbles and cocaine outside of the McDonald's, looking flippant and regal like how it feels to turn into yourself

ABBEY LINCOLN: "YOU CAN'T REALLY TELL THE STORY UNTIL EVERYONE GETS ON THE STAGE."

Eugenics on Fifth and Lennox

We muttered the words S U G A R   H I L L until they made a praise chant

What are we celebrating?

Slaves still in the swamp harvesting cane today Big Daddy Kane's bling is
hollow and wade in the water is still a relevant lament. More slaves died
for sugar than niggas die for one another more slaves went under for sugar
than for cotton, you could pray over the cotton and program it safe but
the sugar water alone much less full of shit and blood and moaners

Safety is a pathetic notion to a black body   The same boy who was rapping
about roaches invading his generic cereal boxes in the projects last week, is
in Soho this week claiming he's never tasted the slaves who tasted the sugar
they made of him even as they whisper mercies across his burden—

I am shrinking a heap of cherries so shiny and ruby they reflect me,
glimmer when I blink a sudden puppy steals the seeds and crams them
into the grass desperately more will grow there and reflect that teeming
how our black genome is hilariously impossible to defeat but every
time you crave a taste of that white powder picked in a field you can't
see by a nigga you can't save on an island you believe is a resort every
time you pretend cake is a casual delicacy   and   smear that blood into
parties I wish you the deepest   enlightenment   Yoruba   you rub off
sweetawfulblues

"They're not forcing me to do s***. I'm just gonna stay black and die. Why, because I'm
black? So every time something happens because I'm black I gotta stand up? What the
f*** am I, Al Sharpton now? I'm A$AP Rocky. I did not sign up to be no political activist. I
wanna talk about my motherf***' lean, my best friend dying, the girls that come in and
out of my life, the jiggy fashion that I wear, my new inspirations in drugs!

I don't wanna talk about no f*** Ferguson and s*** because I don't live over there! I live
in f**** Soho and Beverly Hills. I can't relate. I'm in the studio; I'm in these fashion
studios; I'm in these b***s' drawers. I'm not doing anything outside of that. That's my
life."

With a joy that cuts so deep it is qualitatively different than pleasure /

Everything I ever wanted

Some chicken at noon
that criminal ocean
some noon chicken at noon
some chicken come noontime
black potential   so scratchy, sun
we mesmerize and keep glamouring lean
supple blooming tom-tom possibilities   even / eve 'n them
hunt something new to our situation, some chicken
some noon-noon ness tree chicken crooners for whom
violence becomes confidence   the con charm of martyrs is   some of em are
    polite suicides
the black male leader ones, unaware duty from   selenium to lumbar remembers
humiliation as a large chicken hung in the memory to spell rebirth backwards, three
hurry birds but that was a movie   shoulders back neck free, your co-star is
allergic to watermelon, soft song plunged up from the guillotine as when the joy of
opposites is a flesh unto itself

Lee Perry is babbling again   how I am the sky computer/ mute entropy scene in
which he go 360 and Miles, he's trapped in furs   and bitter whispers and
Nat's rage lurks in blind echoes   make showtunes of slave roads
We will not be coerced into struggling by our taste for blood   and conversation yet

and besides   we don't eat flesh   and yet   abidingly   I'm everything
I ever wanted   I promise   to get light

STARDUST FROM TOMORROW

The way Sun Ra let his performances begin has almost nothing to do with the Western musical tradition. In the Far East, a NÙ-play will often open – as circumstances dictate – in a big unpredictable chaos, yet rigorous discipline is one of the premises of the NÙ-play. Who ever has seen/ heard Sun Ra's concerts will not find this phenomenon unfamiliar. Opening ceremonies for festivities in African village squares share this openness of form, which is unknown to the Western concept of music and theatre. The relations between public and performers are manifold. Sun Ra's concert openings were always rituals of beginning. Thereby he took a measure of existing conditions – in relation to the public, his own dates of life, cosmic constellations, the space and time of the concert and the individual dispositions of the musicians. The Arkestra dressed in the colours which related to the cosmic condition of the moment.

MYSTERY INTRO is one of those beginnings. A ritual as a montage of various openings. Drums and percussion instruments start. After a pause, Tyrone Hill's trombone joins them, then Nascimento Santos establishes the basic rhythm. Freely improvising, other instruments interfere until Michael Ray skips in with his bopish trumpet in a quite unexpected fast swinging rhythm. June Tyson and Michael Ray invoke the word "mystery"; the magic of language is Alpha and Omega both in Sun Ra's song texts and in his philosophical writings. The basic rhythm adjusts to the rhythm of the word 'mystery'– on top of it Marshall Allen's alto shouts with joy. Mysterious combinations of sound from bassoon and bass clarinet follow. Through the reaction of the public one can almost see the battle between Ray and Hill, as they chase each other with their instruments across the stage. The sound wanders through the room. The microphone has no function left but to document. After a short tutti, Julian Priester enters with a filigree-like solo on his trombone. Up to this point Sun Ra has hardly been heard, but one has noticed his handwriting in the conducting. In the tutti, which concludes the MYSTERY INTRO, the accents, glissandi and entries are controlled by special conducting signs – some by the tiniest finger movements. In these parts the harmonic material is ad libitum.

Dreaming and Responsibility

You wish to be responsible for everything except your dreams. What miserable weakness. What lack of logical courage. Nothing contains more of your own work than your dreams.

NEW TORCH SINGER
IS EX-CHOIR MEMBER

NEWEST success-
bound entertainer
to emerge from the
ranks of choir singers is
torch songstress Anna
Marie, 23-year-old Chi-
cago born lass whose
night-club career started
her to stage a show in
Jackson, Mich., for teen-
agers. Musicians who
heard her sing recom-
mended her, soon thereafter
Marie found herself
singing in Los Angeles.

Until ... lemme start loving myself the sure way
Reefer and ice and some sluggish I got a right to
sing the blues
Naked on stage and in my imagination, when are you gonna
understand
All we do is pray and prove the shit you wanna ignore is all the things you are
He walked off stage in the wrong direction
In the middle of a set full of his best black shit   Sinatra laughed like a whip
Reminded him of Dixie whistling mingled with Georgia snow   cotton negro
king   loaded on coke and whips
                    Whippin a Range

Whippin an Escalade   with   lazy   rims say, you reckon I   weep into the
microphone like a home man   ass whippin backstage nigga   crying   crayon
blue   I used to love yous

          'told him to turn around and cross in the right direction

Who told him
you, who?

Neurotic nonchalance not ours   maybe? Whose?

Church marquee says God's   maybe   doctrinaire Jesus maybe   zoot
parade maybe

I'm not going back out on that stage   maybe   not   a blues for Richard
Pryor   maybe a riot where we burn   through the right side of town   this
time   etch a path around   the afterlife   aggressively distant   faux
suede ballet flats, then get distracted in that spotlight

See *how nature can expose a nigga*

In any case my body makes the sentences. Now I'll never know which bruises you gave me and which ones I made myself, running through our melted rehab looking for green grapes. Leaping into limp air to soar past the famous graves. Is salvation that laugh you hear coming closer when Alice Coltrane plays Mantra for John. He beat her to it. That was rude and chivalrous. Those were horses and fists in his eyes and remorse and a child, goodbye. This is a world full of sociopaths and when you change, liar. This world is only love but most men love backwards. Did he beat me, too? I want to ask my mother. Am I lovable. Am I part of the tribe, screamer. I don't remember any pain. How do we get any closer unless we cause one another pain? I don't remember

It used to make me dream faster ™

I'm looking for all to be rendered

I'm looking for all to come about from my soul

Mr. HUGHES. Could I ask you, sir, which books of mine are in the libraries?

Senator DIRKSEN. They are here, and I think we will probably refer to a number of them.

Mr. HUGHES. I see, because I could not quite know otherwise.

Mr. COHN. We will refer you from time to time to specific ones. Let me ask you this: Have you ever been a Communist?

Mr. HUGHES. No, sir. I presume by that you mean a Communist party member, do you not?

Mr. COHN. I mean a Communist.

Mr. HUGHES. I would have to know what you mean by your definition of communism.

Mr. COHN. Have you ever been a believer in communism?

Mr. HUGHES. I have never been a believer in communism or a Communist party member.

Mr. COHN. Have you ever been a believer in socialism?

Mr. HUGHES. My feeling, sir, is that I have believed in the entire philosophies of the left at one period in my life, including socialism, communism, Trotskyism. All isms have influenced me one way or another, and I can not answer to any specific ism, because I am not familiar with the details of them and have not read their literature.

Mr. COHN. Are you not being a little modest?

Mr. HUGHES. No, sir.

Mr. COHN. You mean to say you have no familiarity with communism?

Mr. HUGHES. No, I would not say that, sir. I would simply say that I do not have a complete familiarity with it. I have not read the Marxist volumes. I have not read beyond the introduction of the Communist Manifesto.

Mr. COHN. Let us see if we can get an answer to this: Have you ever believed in communism?

Mr. HUGHES. Sir, I would have to know what you mean by communism to answer that truthfully, and honestly, and according to the oath.

Mr. COHN. Interpret it as broadly as you want. Have you ever believed that there is a form of government better than the one under which this country operates today?

Mr. HUGHES. No, sir, I have not.

Mr. COHN. You have never believed that?

Cyclical Model of the Omniverse

Alright, now I'm gonna seem like I'm changing the subject, but I'm actually not changing/the subject. There were two migrations of the pantheistic deities from their origins. One was toward the apotheosis and one toward the human's purpose, to express consciousness in the biosphere. Now we combine both and celebrate the hybrid. To start, imagine a party where nobody cares how good or bad anybody looks 'cause we are all too busy enjoying ourselves.

A demigod called Shiva is among the guests. She's even forgotten her own name and dances to the reach of its memory. And as long as Shiva dances, the universe, with all of its rules and regulations and conventions, continues to endure as it is. But when Shiva stops dancing, the whole thing implodes, the whole universe constricts into whatever it was before the big bang. And everything is calm and black and there is nothing. And then Shiva starts dancing again and it's all returning but from the beginnings and brand new scenarios but the same everlasting whole. And we're told that Shiva is about truth and eternity, soul and soul again. But the truth part is really hard because when you get beyond the world of illusion and see everything in its beauty and concrete particularity, you also see the world for what it is and we are all so deeply, deeply imperfect. We know that human beings are really a sorry lot indeed, and yet we have the capacity to do this stuff, to see the world both close up and at a distance because we're also deeply deeply perfect and renewable too. So the truth in her movements makes Shiva an outsider. Which is how she remembers her name. She's the one who comes into the community, which is rigidly compressed and tradition-bound and seduces everybody's husband and breaks up all these families and then runs off into the forest. And they run after her and try to hurt her because she's upset all these frantically stable life forms. However it's not so easy to hurt Shiva, since she is also the embodiment of asceticism and healing. The one who sees who we are from the perspective that is greater than ourselves so that she is no longer embedded in the rules and traditions and ego trips that we use to give our lives meaning. And she tries to awaken us to this perspective as an act of generosity and of courage. And anyways we need her to keep dancing

3,000 WILL BURN NEGRO

Kaiser Under Stronger Guard Following Escape Of Crown Prince

Frank Simonds
Writes For States
NEW ORLEANS STATES

From the Jackson, Miss., Daily News, Thursday, June 26, 1919.

NEGRO JERKY AND SULLEN

7th YEAR   Other Trees

New window tint designed to prevent police brutality

At the very start I must warn the reader that we may not share an understanding of such common words as oracle, god, gods, deities, angels, spirits, niggas, negus, nigggahs, beauty, will, spirit, soul, mind, omniverse, individual, food, hood, understanding, subconscious, honkey, perm, magic, miracle, success, law, grace, race, thinking, beliefs, analysis, synthesis, religion, meditation, Wakisha Wilson, Trayvon Martin, Troy Davis, animal, emotions, harmony, consciousness, human, hasbeen, womb, ghost, vampire, soloist, cannibal, master, jazz, jaws, tabloid, entertainer, laugh, cattle, clown, dad, deed, terror, love, marriage, adultery, sainthood, freedom, discipline, needle, polygamy, gun, money, and many, many, many other words, and unless we get on the the same page regarding the meaning of these terms and their related objects, and concepts, this work will not be fully useful to the reader.

(If you don't want to serve negroes in your place of business, then do not have negro records on your juke box or listen to negro records on the radio.)

The screaming, idiotic words, and savage music of these records are undermining the morals of our white youth in America.

Don't Let Your Children Buy, or Listen
To These Negro Records

The Afterlife and the Black Didactic:
Seven Modes for Hood Science

in a blue   way

Then I found I needed words again. Then I found I needed something else. I needed people. As instruments. To be part of the cosmic reordering of the universe. To heal the black/diasporic imagination with counterhistories that destabilize the West and make room for a way of life that serves us here or lets us go elsewhere in peace. There are the martyrs we know by heart, who flood our subconscious minds with the satin bow of caution: don't be too good or effective at mobilizing black consciousness unless you have a death wish, *they whisper*. Then there are those who are so effective and advanced and otherworldly that packaging their legacies could uproot Western culture as we know it and leave us in that land where the sun kills questions, where light is painful and disorienting and suspect and ushers in a crisis of vision. These souls force us to ask whether the very root of our thinking and feeling is being manipulated by a pathological desire to belong in structures that will always intend to dislodge or misuse us until we learn to misuse ourselves in their service. This underclass of martyrs and heroes and master teachers makes us uncomfortable and excessively real to ourselves, but they are the natural born moral custodians, crazy enough to tell a unified truth in a culture that rewards dissimulation, and wise enough to never take themselves too seriously or court disciples. They don't need to.

Strobe

I began to miss the light like it really is /getting in between two actions: apathy/ fascination. People get closer and closer to the beauty of their invention and it tramples them. You can get so close you don't need to say a word. It's blurry without being sentimental like a rebellion in the hood. It's perfect without being good.

THEY'RE FULLY RIPE WHEN FLECKED WITH BROWN

One food that almost digests itself

In the process of ripening, the starch is converted into easily assimilable sugars

MODE ONE, Charles Mingus: Just go on your nerve

The spirit is always the first afflicted in the patterned deterioration we name dis/ease. Spirit seizes in the nearing distance, must choose one of two stances: being/nothingness. The black spirit, diasporic from outer space, the cosmos, the unsayable traits of the unknown, traitor to itself on this planet, is universally sick with dissimulation and at the same time triumphant in its incessantly performed healing, having turned suffering into a kind of spectacular wellness, an excellence, a triumphant swell of countermeaning, a con and a come-up. Having turned the word 'ill' into a compliment, a praise, a willful state of grace.

And we aren't casual about much, keep our intensity on the hush, but we casually announce the pathologies of our heroes in the tone of accolades. That Nigga's Crazy! Turns to mean, we love him dearly, he is our hero, he is completely himself. Charles Mingus was crazy. Lazy affirmation. He grew up in Watts in the 1930s in a working class family, son of a stoic military man. His autobiography will tell you he was punished as a young kid for wetting the bed, and teased for being bowlegged, the teasing a mixture of envy and disdain, the punishment his father's fear that he would grow up to be a chump if he couldn't even control his own bladder.

He grew up to be a jazz soldier, his motor skills on the bass likely on par with those of a marxman in the battlefield, his temperament somewhere between bleeding-heart and kill-or-be-killed. Taurus in the Arena of Life. He was in love with music, women, and food, though all seemed subsidiary to the music, and the literacy and elegance it leant to being in space and time. He wanted all black people to know and master that dignity, to regain control over their thinking by way of rhythm-understanding.

He masters the cello, the bass, the English language and its bastard patois situation too, he masters women and meaning production, becomes one of the best composers of black classical music the world has ever known, eats grapes and chicken until the seeds become bones, and he expects to live forever. We expect him to live forever. Supernigga. Forever Living. He is infatuated with Eastern religion as well as psychoanalysis, what the West uses to analog it, he is paralyzed as well as a pathological dancer. He eats and thinks and fucks and loves too damn much. Does too much acid with Timothy Leary. Disdain comes as easy as joy. He enters a constant state of fight or flight propelled by his already compromised adrenal glands and finally the body grows so fatigued and overloaded with meaning that this surplus short circuits everything. In all of this yearning, all of the bouts of overeating, over-thinking, over-feeling, overstanding, getting over, Mingus' nerves short-circuited early, converged in a kind of manic self-abnegating signal breach. His brain stopped telling his body how to be and his muscles began to atrophy. And we forget that certain organs double as muscles and we forget that jazz musicians are athletes, and they forget how to be mules.

If we look at the human body or form as a kind of unique grammar, the place where rhythm and tone converge turns into an endlessly muted scream and even the screamer can't make it better. Formally called Lou Gehrig's (dis/ease), the condition that Mingus acquired or willed that ultimately lead to his complete physical deterioration is described as a neurodegenerative disorder that causes paralysis, weakness, and ultimately respiratory failure. Motor neurons in the brain, specifically those that control voluntary motion, begin to die, and therefore cannot send signals to the muscles to initiate basic movement. The whole physiology eclipses itself.

Military veterans are approximately twice as likely to be diagnosed with the disease as the general public. Mingus is a jazz soldier. The bedwetting in his early life was a sign that he was born with weak kidneys, the result of generations of adrenal trauma. Slave, slave, slave, soldier, play me the strings of my soul, in that order. Of retaining water in the holds of slaveships. See the kid in there on his knees talking into his own clasped hands this way, in the dark, under water. And the kidneys calibrate fluid and also anger, one clench away from danger. And the anger and also the water are switched off and on by hormones that in turn control the adrenal glands which sit right atop the kidneys, chillin, landing. And no one wants to hear that the American dream murders its early anomalies and poster children, the pimps and jazz musicians and batters and battered, one by one.

So we zoom in on a lurid nuance of Charles Mingus. We zoom in a young black or yellow child soldier, son of a negro (they would have called his father then, with disaffected sophistication, general). He's inherited his parents' stress and converted it into intuition and talent, genius, and he's hip enough to pretend he doesn't blame them, to their faces. It could have been different. He wanted it thus. Dying again and again for his sins which he intended as acts of generosity, jubilation in the tone of loss. He was so misunderstood that he became excessively literal. It was this compromise that killed him, this self-translation or double medium or the time he mistook excess for rebellion cause he was tired of being arrested. Sincerity is a killer.

Are you beginning to feel that bleeding should be reciprocal?
What is practical?
What words rhyme with orange and the red red bornagain feeling? Okay? Reject
them? I'm torn. What is property? What is propaganda? What mourning? Wet
morning? Weather seems to end somewhere? Well you just said . . . is tragedy the
highest form of art? Fuck that. True. But it is pretty mutual, beautiful. This storm is.
This blues troop. I can go for that. Ruthlessly. 'Til the real thing comes along

★★★★★ **Turning the Ship Around**
By Simple tool on April 6, 2002

Format: Mass Market Paperback

This smallish paperback book is just possibly the most influential piece of literature written in the
20th century. The topic is revolution, the issues, racism and sexual discrimination, the incident, the
imprisonment of Angela Davis (and many others). There are contributions from some of the most
famous revolutionaries of the 20th century. They did not achieve their goals as stated. However,
what is revolution? The ship of state confronted their movement and changed direction, no doubt
about that. Two overtly racist systems came down, here and in South Africa. On the cover of the
book, you may see a picture of the young Angela, smiling, with the large afro hairdo we have come
to know. May you be forever young.

MODE FOUR:
Abbey Lincoln senses when niggas is redundant

Polygamy is a Black African technology. It is also a health practice. A poetic form and force and civilized. Several trap queens rising. It is the truth alighting souls loved by nature, our divine order, our birthright, our versatility and our discipline, our means of transcending the tropes of pimps, hoes, and adulterers, wives and lovers and husbands, and think of your liver and how every time you lie, your aura, your electromagnetic field, weakens, trusts you less as source. As soul loved by nature. Either/or. By Kierkegard is nothing like Fear and Trembling by the same manchild.

It is not enough to say that the West's smug and dismissive treatment of polyamory and polygamy threatens the Black spirit here; the West's fear of universal love disrupts all love born here, not only black love. The aura of love itself is weaker in this abyss of one-dimensional commitment. In this mental institution we call the civilized world. If you want a new world you need new concepts, Sun Ra grinned once in a lecture. Do we want a new world? Are we satisfied with this one, patterned around our repressed infatuation with death. Given meaning by the very love that we trouble with ultimatum.

Abbey Lincoln wants a new world. She was once *Jet*'s girl of the week. She sings in nightclubs on film and on islands and in Manhattan and Berlin and Paris and in fits of rage and tenderness. She has married the drummer Max Roach who is rumoured to be a pimp and it's possible that when other men look at her while she's on stage singing, his blood runs hot and when they get home the drum is a woman. Her jaw looks tilted. Her eyes keep the calm of someone who has been in quotidian danger, and survived it. She is a new world. She is the new world she is seeking. A genius is the one who is most like herself in the new world she creates and absconds. Just as well.

What she is trying to tell you is that you are a slave. You don't think your own thoughts and your radiance is bought out and splayed across the plasma screens of the boss man. When Abbey escapes her drummer/pimp/husband who taught her how to scream more, she no longer thinks society thoughts. She can hear her own voice again, crying, telling the truth, looping the vigil around the will again. And she informs us that a man in love with more than one woman is actually a stronger more intelligent more powerful and more loving man for it. If he knows how. If he doesn't use it against the women and himself but instead trusts what the body tells him and the heart and mind. And a woman in love with more than one man is a healer. And several healers can come together and make a family. And a family is a fractal not a square.

The Black African fractal family is meant to be its own opulent village, a space wherein no scarcity was ever meant to exist. No need for escape routes or entrapment. And just like it is safer to legalize prostitution because then the men and women who sell sex for a living can be tested and protected, and their clients protected, in the same way it is safer to honor and admit every lover so that all parties are protected and so the psyche is not fragmented between bogus senses of right and wrong. Love is never wrong. White Supremicists taught us to go against our natural penchant for community and openness. What is wrong is to have multiple partners and to only claim one. In West African models of polygamy a man can have as many wives as he can afford. Both financially and spiritually. And he can only afford as many as he needs. They all complement one another and jealousy is ridiculous, really, petty and small, when all of this is happening in the open. Today in the West the average black man has multiple women he loves and pretends otherwise and neglects them as such and in the end loves no one because he rejects himself, does not love himself. It is hideous to observe and even worse to be a part of, remedial at best. Backwards in the very way we accuse Africa of retrograde. Abbey Lincoln needed a man who could let her work in peace. Who would not have to beat her off the stage in the face of her beauty and then run off and pimp a few more for the good measure of his rigged ego. She needed someone stronger and less brute. She needed someone to king who wouldn't make her suffer for it, fearing his own unworthiness.

It is not only men who seek the idyllic openness of a bond with no legally binding contract attached and at the same time yearn to be the objects of devoted love and desire, women also reel in this binary, as Abbey did. As I do. And the primitiveness we fear is our most abiding salvation under the circumstances. To simply avoid sanctimony by not rejecting ourselves. And in the end that kind of freedom brings us home, to cook and clean and work and make love and money and babies together. In the end we love it when niggas is redundant. Acting otherwise is a lie like sweet Lemonade. Drama/charade. Some days we actually wish some sister wife would take the reins so we can get some work done. Others we wanna spend all day in bed feeding him grapes and melon. If Miles hadn't beaten Frances out into the garden, made her quit dancing her lead in West Side Story, made her run to Hollywood and come up on Marlon Brando. If women weren't possessions and men weren't possessed. Abbey look at your shadow, fathom all our saved souls joined to jump the cage.

JAIL JAMAS
The Daring Gift
for MARRIED FOLKS

HICAGO SUN-TIMES ◆ MONDAY, MAY 3, 2004

Polygamy's popularity defies forecasts

'At least I am not hasing up girls,' says one W. African man

The Black Saint and the Sinnerman

Any good magic man can cure the sick sometimes,
and many of them can cast out devils, especially if they've installed the devils in the first place

And I've seen a good bit of weather magic

love your enemies and all that

He wanted to continue by saying that the war on terror has been a failure
so no one puts it into practice   And that about
solves the absolute tyranny of abstract gods

Thank you very much.   Pleasure.

DAKAR, Senegal — Monday and Tuesday are with Mame Seye. Wednesday and Thursday with Khady. Then, Ibrahima Sene, a successful businessman, welcomes his third lawfully wedded spouse, ida — perfumed, coifed and arrayed in her finery — into his bedroom for two nights.

Defying expectations that Western influence and urbanization would gradually do away with plural marriages, polygamy is going strong across much of Muslim West Africa. In Senegal, nearly 47 percent of marriages are multiple like Sene's.

"At least I am not chasing up girls, or committing adultery," says Sene, 60, sitting on the sofa across from the family's master bed. Two of his wives, flanking im on the couch, nod.

Sene built his house as a bachelor more than three decades ago,

Ibrahima Sene, a successful businessman, is pictured with his first wife, Mame Seye (from left); second wife, Khady, and third wife, Aida, at his house in Dakar, Senegal. –AP

keeping in mind his future spouses and Quranic dictates: Take no more wives than you can deal with justly.

Today, Sene's three wives each have separate apartments in the luxurious villa of high ceilings and marble floors.

At night, the wives often gather in their husband's room to watch TV, before two retire to bed, leaving just one behind.

"Polygamy is in the mind," Sene says, his wives signaling agreement. "Those who have not experienced it don't know anything about it, and therefore criticize it."

AP

MODE FIVE: Mos Def is Trapped in Capetown with His Name on Swell and No Nation

Worldstar had called. The CIA had called. The daughters of the revolution had called. Prank drawl. Baby Momma number etcetera had called. Leverage is also static at that frequency, the frequency of their muted calling. Black Unity by Pharoah Sanders meets Going to Meet the Man by James Baldwin. What would motivate a famous black musician, actor, dreamer, from Brooklyn with wives and children and all American dreams and demons and angels, to renounce it all and move to Capetown, South Africa. Militancy or Bohemianism. Escapism or is he a refugee? And what does it mean to renounce your U. S. passport and citizenship in the name of sovereignty and creative freedom. Is it a stunt and he's about to scream uncle or are you niggas really so programmed by U. S. imperialism that you think this place is safe for your heroes. There's a picture of him wearing a griot kilt, and another of him in handcuffs. In that order. In that danger. Border/range. Love is a dangerous necessity. Next, he is singing a ballad about the penny arcade. He is in a courtroom with three wives at his side. He is on Kanye's answering machine, crying, retiring. Remember when he wore the orange jumpsuit and let them insert a feeding tube down his esophagus to protest the torture of prisoners in Guantanamo? And how ever since he's been in exile?

Speechlessness

Don't talk about the half of our fathers you buried in those samples and I won't

talk about the time I caught you walking out of the club with that muppet-looking white girl

eyes bulging when you saw me like I was a 5-0 flashlight.

Fortress.

I can't get over that.

It was so exactly America that night

I forgot my mother's name that night as I screamed for it

Where am I

MODE SIX: White Pussy Porn and the Niggas who Watch It with their Black Girlfriends

We must never forget what we endeavor to forget   there's another one   bobbing
on my desktop   sent across spacetime   by a nigga, not mine, but   my   nigga   but
not mine   claim numb, claim no one   next he'll send a ghetto concerto   next
another loop of a white man and a white woman fucking with foundation and mascara
all over their faces   both of them   vaseline on their teeth, velvet robes covering the
backs of their cloth and oak dressing room chairs   next   a blotted ballad   dipped in
his cum and stolen moments   and one gif titled little nigger girl gets white dick   it
is best to be literal about these things ripping open the internet   no I won't vote for
Hillary Clinton, no I won't forget   how she must have suffered over her husband's love
of blow jobs, not at all, she did not suffer, the other woman suffered, suffering women
will vote for her, next an excerpt from Red Desert the movie, with English subtitles,
next a picture of me on my knees with his dick in my mouth, Nigga money listen,
caramel Monica Vitti, channeling, we are brown or something, I'm the golden echo, I
glow here on my knees in the dark, almost praying, and am needed in the boardroom
to explain the role of mitochondrial DNA in all this remembering— smiling enslaved
Africans carrying bales of cotton and the lady who played the gangster's wife for so
long and I, hope to run this freedom off a cliff and let it wake up on the cross trapped in
a sex tape looking for watermelon with black seeds in it, all over L.A. Bill Cosby went
blind today. #ofabloodlessrevolution

MK Beta was the CIA's sex slave program. Create a new
personality in a woman and program her to become a sex slave,
or in most instances, a celebrity.

Every song in the western world is a protest song; like worrying that comes true, so, alright, fine, I'm worried I'm gonna win or worse, pass, and I don't know what game that is you

called a heart

polyphasic as you are
why I
sleep and why I don't

Why the Black Panthers were recruiting at Newport

And the black was not redundant

There were all these kinds of one to land on the path to a fitness fit for television, you must be--

which still isn't betrayal until you notice and keep going

MODE SIX: Your Mukbang Made Me Weep

A morbidly obese black boy named Jasper sits at his dormitory desk with three buckets of hot wings and turns on his camera, presses record, begins eating wings and talking into the camera, about the food and how he's living. He is making a Mukbang or 'eating show' that he will upload to Youtube; it receives 500,000 views in the first week. Fame/scene. I see how this could kill me, he jokes, about a particularly hot piece of dripping wet wing meat. Survivor's guilt. For forty-five minutes he eats for us. Performs hunger and satiation. Emblems longing and retreat. Is this a song. Is he singing. Watching in a soft trance, I feel like he's singing for me, to me, a blues— he intends to program my desire into solidarity with his. But I feel no hunger, no longing, no retreat, no satisfaction. I am a part of a numb landscape in which his performance takes shape, a passive enabler. We coexist. Who does the fetish object fetishize? Men watch women eat dick night after night, women watch men devour wings. Now who's flying. Now you get to watch a Korean woman eat Obama Fried Chicken, live from Seoul. Apollo Amateur Night: Be good or be gone, style-eating. Crucial to a successful Mukbang is the volume of food. There must be so much it seems impossible for one person to finish, and by the end, only piles of bones and oilslicks this papier ocean. The eating show must mimic the killing field, casually, we are at war with our desire and the chicken isn't winning, and we aren't winning, the act itself is winning, bare bones and dimples. I watch him eat and chat for forty-five minutes, quiet tears a burning tree, a glowing screen, two free Americans at the new virtual dinner table and out of irony. Desire unfolding as exhibition. This is an actual experience. This is real life. Unreality is not my muse. Jasper is beautiful. In the Heat of the Night. When he slaps that white cop at the empty train station in Memphis. I love watching him do this. Hallucination, get loose with the new food. I rewind and watch again. I am hungry and he feeds me these images while I suck the last flesh from a mango seed. While the badge falls onto the tracks, is flattened into beats. While we weep and laugh, free at last. *Now that's charisma!*

I step into my father's solitude and it works. Now we share a big idea together. A Harmony in infinite parts- How a visionary is a caller of light, one who summons spirits that heal. How there is no other reason than this, to make music or to live

MODE SEVEN:
The State of New York vs. Alfredo Bowman

How much of your identity is wrapped up in your death drive. How much does belief govern the way you age and live? You believe in your deterioration and thus will it, villain to your own endless self. How much does your desire to leave this place demand fried chicken and other scandalous shit? Do you live under a spell of excuses to die too young? Are you the wasted swell of immortality on the Christian sands of I wanna be ready? Ready to put on that long white robe.

Alfredo Bowman was killed in prison for curing AIDS.

Alfredo Bowman smoked weed everyday.

Alfredo Bowman is your hero.

Alfredo Bowman is Dr. Sebi, he saved your life, he died for your sins.

Alfredo Bowman is the black man born in 1933 and raised in Honduras, who received no formal education but went on to be a merchant seaman, travel the globe, make good money, develop diabetes and obesity in the throes of it all, recover with the help of herbs and a master herbalist from Mexico, and apply the principles he discovered in the process to cure AIDS, Parkinson's, blindness, all forms of cancer, every so-called disease you can name or conjure. The first step in his cure was repudiation, the innerstanding that there is no such thing as disease, in the way we imagine, there is only obstruction of the lymphatic fluid which eventually poisons the blood or robs it of minerals and creates the abnormal cells we call sickness. And the obstruction is not the boogie man hiding in the body waiting to reap, nor some inevitable genetic defect, it is the accumulation of waste and undigested matter from food and other toxic substances we willingly consume, food and drink that is too acidic for the human body and causes it to create excess mucus to protect itself from being chewed up by acid. When the colon, kidneys, and skin are overloaded and can't eliminate the poison as quickly as you are taking it in, the self immolation begins, the tonsils, the thyroid, the appendix maybe, go down first, as warning, and if you still don't heed the body's cry for help, if it's hedonism or else, the cells start to mutate, cluster, harden into cysts and tumors, and turn on themselves because you've trapped them in a burning ghetto in the name of status quo convenience or desire or cause you don't know how to live, obsessed with a culture carved out of the crumbs of your oppressor. You've fed your cells cow hormones when they needed human ones, stuffed them with the rotting meat of other animals when they craved chlorophyll and a candid sun.

The body is a benevolent vessel that wants to behold the true self so badly it will evict you if it has to, render your spirit inadmissible so it can carry on in truth, or suffocate you in the mucus of your robotic decisions until you change.

Alfredo Bowman discovered all of this and became Dr. Sebi. He opened a healing center in Honduras where he cured AIDS as well as scores of equally devastating conditions using herbs and thermal waters sourced from deep within the ground. In 1987 his mother suggested he take an ad out in the *Village Voice* announcing: AIDS has been cured. Sebi was obedient and respected his mother more than anyone on earth, so followed her advice like a reverent, son. Two months later he was arrested and thrown in jail in Manhattan. When his case came to trial, the State of New York vs. Alfredo Bowman, he hired no lawyer, he defended himself barefoot and in layman's terms, and won. Seventy Seven patients whose diseases he had reversed including several former AIDS patients showed up in court with the diagnostic sheets, proving they had once been sick and were now among the healthiest people you can find in the modern world thanks to Alfredo Bowman, Dr. Sebi, and his herbal compounds and dietary recommendations. There was no denying Sebi's authenticity. There was no way to invoke Western science, which had failed all of Sebi's patients, as offense for the state. This was in 1987. Now it's the year 2016.

Since that pivotal supreme court case so-called diseases have been no less prevalent and the practitioners of allopathic medicine are still looking for cures and antidotes everywhere but in the kitchen and the garden, while the business that our collective bad or numb habits creates for Western doctors is booming. What about Tuskegee, and Henrietta Lax, and Anarcha, tortured property of James Marion Sims. Despite these and countless other horrors inflicted on black bodies by so-called doctors, we trust Western medicine and the psychology that comes with it. Sanitation employees in hazmat gear are paid thousands a day to discard hazardous medical waste, the same waste they inject into your body as vaccines, chemotherapy, radiation, amalgam fillings, x-rays, gamma-rays, raising the pitch of your suffering. And Dr. Sebi's protocols and compounds are still curing patients allopathy turns away or undermines with harsh, hopeless treatment. This is not glorified voodoo, this is the work of a man who understands the glory of simplicity. Eat the food that comes from the earth, drink the water that comes from the spring, take the herbs meant for healing, not adulterated chemicals and animal flesh. Somehow the doctrine of success in the West treats triumphs like Sebi's as rock bottom Bohemianism, too restrictive to be natural, food shrinkwrapped and packaged like toys is received as more palatable than what comes right from the ground, and the Sebis of the world are treated as mythic archetypes who harness some ancient magic or dumb luck, rather than honored as healers and souls loved by nature.

In August of 2016 Alfredo Bowman died somewhere between the prison he was placed in and the hospital they were rushing him to. They, who? He was in jail for carrying cash he would have used to purchase herbs. Thirty Seven thousand dollars, the I Ching number for the clan, the family, mafia at your feet, a modest sum to invest in plants. Fifty alternative healers have been found dead in this same calendar year. A coke dealer somewhere in Manhattan just spent that same sum on white powder you might snort up your nose job. Sebi had been behind bars for nearly two months and was due to be released a couple of days from the day his killing was complete. He died like Sandra Bland, he died like my father, somewhere between prison and transcendence. There was no autopsy in Sebi's case. No explanation. His healing center in Honduras and his headquarters in Los Angeles remain active. He is survived by 17 children. In the last video footage of him he is seen sitting on the concrete outside of an airport, knees beneath his chin, head bowed in prayer. You will not see his name anywhere mainstream. You will see the muting of his legacy and more commercials for toxic pharmaceuticals that end in whispered lists of side effects far worse than anything they treat. We lost a savior in August. AIDS was cured in 1987. A black man named Alfredo Bowman, aka Dr. Sebi, cured AIDS, cancer, diabetes, self-loathing, shame, super-market deceit. Do you expect your oppressor to save you, too?

Herbalist found not guilty in 'fake' healing case
HAROLD JAMISON
New York Amsterdam News 1963-1993; Oct 1, 1988;
ProQuest Historical Newspapers New York Amsterdam News: 1922-1993
pg. 3

Herbalist found not guilty in 'fake' healing case

By HAROLD L. JAMISON

In a historical decision in Brooklyn Supreme Court Monday, a jury of six men and six women found Alfredo Bowman not guilty on two counts of practicing medicine without a license.

Bowman, affectionately known as Dr. Sebi, director of USHA Herbal Research Institute, 810 Fulton St., Brooklyn, was arrested Feb. 10, 1987, by Attorney General Robert Abrams' office Immorales placed in the Village Voice and the Amsterdam News, claimed a cure for AIDS.

Bowman's attorney, Sebi's attorney stated this was the first case of its kind in Brooklyn's Supreme Court.

"What was significant about

the verdict," Greenaway stated, "is the fact that USHA's African Bio-Mineral Balance will now be recognized throughout the world."

DR. SEBI
...to heal itself.

described the African Bio-Mineral Balance "as a dietary program that is consistent with the African genetic structure."

The dietary program consists of natural herbal compounds, fresh fruits, vegetables and juices.

According to Sebi's testimony, "the compounds change the environment of the body through intercellular cleansing and replacing the cells by treating cell proliferation, wherein new cells push out the old cells."

"This process washes the body

[...] agents, Gail Maltz and Michael Colon were wired with a small tape recorder. The tape recording, submitted into evidence by Barclay, failed to survive the jury that Sebi did in fact make a medical diagnosis. One agent's testimony, under cross examination by Greenaway, clearly stated that he did not receive the response from Sebi that would constitute a medical diagnosis.

A questionnaire used by Sebi to ascertain the health of clients was submitted in evidence by the prosecution to support his contentions that Sebi and the

Greenaway described USHA's concept of natural healing as one "as a sufficient course with the medical establishment."

[...] patients were practical medicine. However, this disputed by testimony of Joanne Theirs-Pockette, a former USHA employee who used the questionnaire to fill out the questionnaire to ascertain the health of clients, and collect fees for several purposes.

Harry Dotson Roper Sebi, Samuel Fuller, Dalia and Karen Kelly, witnessed the defense, emphatically lifted to their improved health as a result of USHA's dietary program.

And are you whistling the same jive as them?

EVERY RACE

Under the rubric of performance, every umbrellaed Jesus joins the antebellum picnic. And in that case, it is really about desire. What we are allowed to want. The boundaries our identities place on these desires, wants, needs. Also what we are allowed to believe and think. Whole gaps in origin mythology that we never peer into on account of our performed amnesia. Did slaves eat animal flesh upon arriving here on those filthy Western ships? No. Massa had to go back for okra and fonio grain. Did sex feel good in captivity? I watched my black father choke my white mother when the greens weren't tender, enough. Later on they cuddled and watched Beau Bridges gentrify Park Slope. Did Western doctors learn surgical procedures by first performing them on unanesthetized slaves? Yes. Did they dose their enslaved subjects up with morphine to prevent insurrection? Yes. What is epigenetics? So you mean those memories are passed down in our DNA, coding, a kind of biological intelligence so we know what to do in captivity? But what about freedom? Does that mean we keep repeating the same cycle except now we associate advanced volunteered slavery with prestige and success with living like our mentally ill captors?

A quick list of black owned strip clubs goes here.

With all those cow hormones running through our veins we're sure to catch a dollar between the lines.

Trapped in the second hand glamor of your casual bad habits   you feel free in this gridded city, drunk and so pretty at the pizza parlor with a swarm of suitors watching you eat the pyramid. That milk of the cow and the blood of the cow   and pus and disease   and nightshade   made natural   as an open mouth under this powdered   starlight.   All the thankless labor that goes into these triumphant American scenes makes your spirit so ugly. But in the moment it feels very beautiful   and free. Like escaping something through being watched   seen, surveilled, normal! Look at me   I'm black   I've suffered tremendously and I can eat flesh late   at night like   my body is a suburb, like my body is a ghetto gone hunting. I am a thriving well adjusted college graduate.   The only habit I question is thinking.   Subterrestrial burdens looser,   looser—   Let go of your mother's neck. Tight grip on the dream they sold you. I had a dream they sold me.   As though the synergy that gives life meaning can be accessed through a series of minor transgressions disguised as freedom   the good life   at what price   a dollar a slice ? Phat black asses flailing in the moonlight like this / a magic cotton field

But then where do we bury the questions killed by our benevolent sun

—a brilliant maniac the sun must feel like, out there on stage every day trying to save us from the hunt for meaning. The futility becomes not that it isn't there (the meaning) but that it's all there, it's all illuminated, until a primitive indifference to everything that burns under its gaze must make that radiance feel a bit blasé, but no less lucid. I thought I'd cured the abyss/ I'd only exceeded it and turned into this avid speaker between me and my own listening, a point of access to the subconscious that then needs to be toned in order to avoid excess seeing (over-vulnerability) or blindness (delusion). Most everything becomes symbolic and mundane in that newborn haven of an abyss, and most of all . . . anything that could last through all that silence, deserves the name love/ I once underestimated the capacity of my own, heart, soul, and spirit, now I spend the abyss forgiving myself, not quite Dionysus but not quite anything else either. It seems perfectly natural to assume that I have always existed. The phone rings. I'm accidentally calling myself from my computer. I still have the strength to laugh. You still lack the strength to cry and when you discover it don't take it for granted. Yes, that's love.

THE INSIDIOUS PLOT BY OBAMA TO ELIMINATE WHITE PEOPLE THROUGH CLIMATE CHANGE (VIDEOS)

JULY 18, 1974/50¢   A JOHNSON PUBLICATION

JET

Look for me in the whirlwind

She teaches us that voodoo was used as a means, during slavery, for slaves to break free from the slave master. When the slave wanted to break free from the master, the only way to get out a lot of times was to die. That's right, to die. And they had an antidote in voodoo that would cause the body to stop, the heart to stop, and all that, the consciousness to leave the body and move to the nervous system, and the slavemaster would just come to check to see that the slave was dead, check the pulse or whatever, and let the slaves bury them, but the family would be in and knowing that nah, he's not dead, or she's not dead. We're just faking out master, so we can get him or her off the land, so that they can go get us some help so we can break free from the plantation.

What really happened to Prince, Dr. Sebi, Malcolm, Michael Jackson   Don't be paranoid but here's a pair of bells   and a come back as   manual

Where   are the Niggas   who know   about statelessness   and still wear dazed Nikes   with a three piece   Are we marvelous

           is this our value   less   the escape   route ?

Good Time People

The first time I heard the word Africa and knew it loved us   was struggling to reach us and love us,   would exploit every tragedy in the business to reveal its trouble/joy   we were in that battered women's shelter in blueblack Iowa rural hush to the authority of our curses   me and mama and her nine months' belly pretending the elevator was our flight to California, hearing the slanted beat of a tambourine between floors and cots and wounded bodies, redemption chore choir in the water with the lights shy flickering in the hide-and-seek mannerisms of refugees, hiding from who we longed for. For a lifetime. And the one ally we made in our shelter, Mr. Williams, round and brown and longed for, would close his eyes in the middle of a story about our impending Hollywood freedom/I'm waiting. He would drift off to his standing sleep before giving away the meaning. African Sleeping Sickness, he called it. Where was that. Why was the sickness theirs and so far away. Why was he the best at solving our case, in his sleep. Break down the grace of luck. Where was his gun, I wondered. Where was his agony to match. How did he plan to fight it. Was he anything like us, runner. Like me and my father and my future. What was he doing to keep from living this other man's dream. Our first and most modern Sisyphus, redeemer, redentor, casual healer, recalled in the field of my perfect nightmare on earth, you mean, I could have just slept through all this, could just turn the suffering into the dream, live happily ever after in California?

Planet Nibiru? Mysterious Sphere Over California ... - The Inquisitr
www.inquisitr.com/.../planet-**nibiru**-mysterious-sphere-over-california-arkansas-and-s... ▾
Jun 18, 2015 - A mysterious sphere that appeared in the skies over the U.S. and South **Africa** last week sparked speculations that Planet X/**Nibiru** had arrived ...

Africa Archives - Nibiru Today
nibirutoday.com › Nibiru Visible ▾
Apr 3, 2016 - UFO & **Nibiru** Winged Disk Sun at NIGHT! Planet X Update... Home **Nibiru** Visible **Africa**. Latest. Latest · Featured posts · Most popular · 7 days ...

Planet Nibiru? Mysterious Sphere Over California ... - Before It's News
beforeitsnews.com/.../planet-**nibiru**-mysterious-sphere-over-california-arkansas-and-s... ▾
Jun 18, 2015 - A unexplainable sphere that showed up in the skies over the U.S. and South **Africa** last week resulted in speculations that Planet X/**Nibiru** had ...

Nibiru's Projected Path from 2011 – 2018? | Heaven Awaits
https://heavenawaits.wordpress.com/**nibiru**-projected-path-from-2011-2018/ ▾
The pictures of **Nibiru** presented here cannot be associated with the path of... ... So every observatory in Australia, South America, **Africa** and India should be ...

Video of Nibiru rising in Africa – Villagers say presence of God ...
investmentwatchblog.com/video-of-**nibiru**-rising-in-**africa**-villagers-say-presence-of-g... ▾
Jul 4, 2016 - It appears to be a rainbow at first glance ... In this video you will see Planet X Rising and looming huge in the daytime sky as the entire village ...

Funny how things can get away from you   for years you can't remember anything   and then one day it all comes back

And despair   can abandon   us but hope can't   when   prisoners don't own their own images so   all the new stars   got   bars   and bards to tell it are so out of style   like   motors   and Sunday

          believe me, mama,

  The true   ugly   thing is the pretending   like martyrs   and Sunday

we see our names   to trees   and set them easy   on   fire   til we   can   mutter   the

                              effigies   as flight

Trains do something to black   people   just   wanna   runaway ,   right

Roland Kirk be like   *here comes the whistle man*

I be like   precious lord, take my hand   lead me   on

SAINT JOHN COLTRANE
AFRICAN ORTHODOX CHURCH
JURISDICTION OF THE WEST

Reparations begin in the body™

Effective social bonds for 500

toward a land where the sun kills questions I mean where

everything

she calls herself throwing shade

feels like a mandate   as you make your way   into that light

BREAKING NEWS

ARCHBISHOP FRANZO W. KING D.D. FOUNDER
1286 FILLMORE STREET, SAN FRANCISCO, CA. 94115
WWW.COLTRANECHURCH.ORG